LEAN

QuickStart Guide

SECOND EDITION

The Simplified Beginner's Guide to Lean

Benjamin Sweeney

in partnership with

Edition #2: Created January 2, 2017

Cover Illustration and Design: Katie Poorman, Copyright © 2016 by ClydeBank Media LLC
Interior Design: Katie Poorman, Copyright © 2016 by ClydeBank Media LLC
Editors: Marilyn Burkley & Bryan Basamanowicz

All Rights Reserved

Printed in the United States of America

Publisher's Cataloging-In-Publication Data
(Prepared by The Donohue Group, Inc.)

Names: Sweeney, Benjamin. | ClydeBank Business.
Title: Lean quickstart guide : the simplified beginner's guide to lean /Benjamin Sweeney, in partnership with ClydeBank Business.
Description: Second edition. | Albany, NY : ClydeBank Media, LLC, 2016. | Includes bibliographical references.
Identifiers: LCCN 2016962419 | ISBN 978-0- 9963667-0- 0 | ISBN978-1- 945051-16- 6 (ebook)
Subjects: LCSH: Lean manufacturing. | Industrial efficiency-- Management. | Value analysis (Cost control)
Classification: LCC TS155 .S94 2016 (print) | LCC TS155 (ebook) | DDC658.5-- dc23

ClydeBank Media LLC
P.O. Box 6561
Albany, NY 12206

www.clydebankmedia.com

ISBN-13: 978-0-9963667-0-0

contents

BEFORE YOU START READING, DOWNLOAD YOUR FREE DIGITAL ASSETS!

Be sure to visit the URL below on your computer or mobile device to access the free digital asset files that are included with your purchase of this book.

These digital assets will compliment the material in the book and are referenced throughout the text.

DOWNLOAD YOURS HERE:

www.clydebankmedia.com/lean-assets

Introduction

The Lean model for production and manufacturing is a collection of business practices, strategies, and methods that focus on *waste* elimination and continuous improvement within an organization. Often referred to simply as "Lean," this business model has applications in every industry, not just the world of manufacturing. All businesses, and many organizations outside the business world, can benefit from Lean's rigorous and vigilant approach to waste reduction and efficiency.

Lean is a management philosophy with a holistic approach that was interpreted from the ***Toyota Production System***, an operations and corporate culture system developed by the popular and highly successful automobile manufacturer, Toyota. At the center of the Lean business concept is the effort to eliminate three types of manufacturing variation and waste: muda, mura, and muri.

Muda represents waste in its most physical form, and it directly translates from Japanese as "futility" or "uselessness." The objective with waste reduction and elimination is to clearly separate the ***value-added*** activities from the activities that are identified as wasteful or ***non-value-added***. Muda is the easiest form of waste to understand. It is what many organizations would traditionally classify as waste: defective production, time spent performing non-value-added activities, unnecessary inventory, etc. These specific forms of waste, as well as several other sources of muda, are identified and outlined in detail in the next section.

Mura is waste in the sense of unevenness. Distinct from muda and muri, mura is less easily quantified, though no less impactful on operations. Unevenness in workflow can result in unnecessary downtimes or periods of unnecessary stress on equipment, systems, and workforce. From a management stance, unevenness creates another element that all business practitioners seek to eliminate: uncertainty. Irregular intervals are difficult to predict, and therefore, forecasting becomes difficult. A high degree of uncertainty can greatly reduce the responsiveness of an organization's supply chain. Mindfulness of mura is essential when determining facility layout or assembly protocol as well as understanding and improving the long-term forecasting abilities and short-term processes for an organization and the ability to respond to fluctuating demand.

Muri is a failure to understand capabilities or to succumb to the effects of overburden. This is a tangible concept when applied to facility layout and assembly and manufacturing processes; too much of a workload on a system can cause failure or increase rates of defective production. Overburden in conjunction with unevenness can also create expensive bottlenecking within an organization. Wear and tear on machines or repetitive strain injuries among the workforce can be reduced or alleviated through ensuring that only value-added activities are being performed, as well as through reduction of waste in other areas.

fig. 1

Muda	Mura	Muri
Manufacturing Waste Events	Unevenness of Workflow	Overburden
Non-Value-Added Activity	Reduces Responsiveness	Reduces Responsiveness
Incurs Cost	Leads to Waste Events	Leads to Waste Events

In conjunction with the overriding value of waste reduction through identification and elimination of muda, mura, and muri lies the philosophy of kaizen, or the creation of a culture of continuous improvement. The concept of kaizen is as powerful as it is versatile and, in practice, can be implemented in a multitude of ways that span diverse industries. ***Kaizen*** is a mindset as much as a business asset, and represents organizational culture more than a set of manufacturing tools. Permeating all levels of the organization, kaizen not only lays the groundwork for the implementation of Lean, but also guides decision-making, innovation, and improvement at both the micro and macro levels. The concept of kaizen is so powerful that even personal trainers and life coaches use similar approaches with the individual lives of clients seeking to better themselves.

Many aspects of the Lean production system build on this common thread of kaizen and rigorous, continuous improvement. As we explore the world of Lean production, the concept of kaizen, if not implicitly stated, will be evident in best practices and prescribed methods.

Though its origins lie squarely in the manufacturing sector, the less tangible aspects of Lean mean that it can be tailored to fit nearly any organization from the service sector, like healthcare firms, insurance agencies, government agencies, and beyond. Since Lean is a blend of keen, structured business improvement insights and efficient, impactful manufacturing tools, organizations in other industrial sectors can stretch the Lean model to fit their operations. In addition to the data-driven and day-to-day productivity tools that are all part of the Lean toolkit, the real power of Lean lies in the creation of a vigilant mindset among the entire workforce, from workers on the assembly line all the way up to the CEO's office, that the elimination of waste, the need for continuous improvement, and the idea that anyone can effect positive change within the organization are essential for a firm's success and longevity.

What follows is a primer on the concepts and ideas that drive the Lean business model and the key components of the winning mindset that keeps contemporary companies on the map.

| 1 |

Six Components of Lean Philosophy

In This Chapter

- The six components of Lean philosophy are explored in detail
- The D.O.W.N.T.I.M.E. sources of waste are illustrated
- The PDCA method and A3 problem solving approach are explored

While the concepts of waste reduction and continuous improvement exist in all aspects of Lean, there are also six primary qualities that organizations should embody to maintain a competitive, responsive, and flexible position within the marketplace. In many cases, management gurus praise to no end the mindfulness of these qualities as keys to a successful business in today's marketplace regardless of their implementation of Lean. Prior to the "leap to Lean," companies should already have a focus on these characteristics in one form or another to establish a solid foundation on which to build the Lean culture. Before the foundational pillars of Lean are addressed, let's look at some basic definitions to better understand the relationship between Lean and value.

At its core, the Lean manufacturing system strives to differentiate between value-added and non-value-added activities. All manufacturing activities incur cost; value-added activities incur cost that can be passed on to the customer. These activities are necessary to produce goods to the customer's specifications, though only these activities will generate results that the customer will pay for.

Any other activities are considered non-value-added, and are classified as waste. Waste events are activities that incur cost, but that do not generate more value, utility, or satisfaction for the customer. A well-known culprit of waste (by any definition) is defective production. When a part is generated with a defect, the customer will not pay for that unit. The manufacturer can't insist that the customer pay just because the manufacturer incurred cost in generating the part; there is no value, and the part must be considered a loss.

A less obvious source of waste is carried *inventory*. There is no value provided to a customer merely because a warehouse has kept units on the shelves for months. Most manufactured goods are the same after a week as after a year, but a year's worth of inventory costs can't simply be added on to each unit that doesn't sell.

Once the differentiation of what constitutes value-added activity and what constitutes waste (non-value-added) is complete, the process of reducing waste can really begin. Visibility leads to action, and sources of waste that are invisible or undetectable will go without remedy indefinitely. A common theme among Lean tools is that their ultimate goal is the detection and exposure of waste. If kaizen is the engine that drives Lean organizations to new heights of efficiency and productivity, then waste reduction is its fuel.

1. Elimination of Waste

As we have discussed, the elimination of waste is a concept central to the Lean framework. While we know that muda, mura, and muri are the three sources of waste within a production cycle, it is necessary to narrow the focus and address each of these sources individually.

Muda is the easiest of the three manufacturing variations to categorize. Almost all of the physical sources of waste within production processes fall into the classification of one of the following eight sources of muda.

Together, the eight sources of waste encompass a very diverse number of individual and unique circumstances and the costs associated with them. While every possible waste event would be impossible to catalog here, this list creates categories used for identifying and addressing waste. The acronym **D.O.W.N.T.I.M.E.** can be used to remember the eight sources of waste.

fig. 2

Defective Production

Defects equal cost and waste. Extra costs may be incurred through reworking, scrap, production rescheduling, or additional labor costs. In some cases defects can more than double the cost of production for a part. Defective production is clearly a non-value-added activity; the cost to produce defective parts cannot be passed on to the customer and must be considered a loss.

Overprocessing

Any time a piece or product receives more processing work than is absolutely required by the customer, it is an overprocessing waste event. While processing to the customer's needs is certainly a value-added activity, customers will not pay more for unnecessary work. Additionally, further processing could result in the creation of new waste events such as wasteful motion, unnecessary waiting, inventory and transportation costs, and the increased risk of defective production.

13

Overprocessing presents a challenge to organizations that do not have a high degree of visibility in the supply chain or have poorly established channels of communication. That is to say that cooperation and coordination are often the obvious remedies for overprocessing waste events. A high level of focus on the customer's needs and customer service, along with communication at all levels of production, are effective methods of eliminating the root causes of overprocessing. Later we discuss the pull production system, another method of combating overprocessing and waste.

Waiting

In circumstances in which goods are not being processed, consumed, or in transport, they are assigned the "waiting" status. Waiting is not a value-added condition and represents a high degree of wasted time and effort that could be better spent on value-added activities.

The elimination of waiting-related waste events is largely based on changes to operations and logistics protocols. Effective plant loading and facility layout, too, can highly impact the amount of time material spends waiting. An effective production system moves goods quickly and efficiently in a steady flow; smart facility layout is the first step in combating the frequency of "waiting" waste events.

Under-Utilized Employee Talent

While the other seven sources of waste have concrete causes, outcomes, and consequences, untapped employee talent is a harder resource to quantify. In many cases, the associated cost is best described as an "opportunity cost" and is difficult to assign a price tag to. Determining when employee talent has been wasted in the first place also comes with challenges, but by using the various elements of Lean an environment can be developed in which employees can flourish and live up to their potential.

While the Lean model provides guidelines for business practices and tactical decisions, it is by no means a method of leadership. All companies would like to be able to say that their managers have a sharp eye for rising talent and that their workforce distribution is the most effective and efficient given its elements. As discussed in the next section, Lean's focus on visibility and creating an environment of continuous improvement can foster an atmosphere in which employees are encouraged to participate. Lean also develops a corporate culture that provides guidance and methods for employees to speak up and incentivizes them to contribute to their fullest potential. If there is an expectation that each and every member of the organization will voice concerns in regard to methods of improvement, then the channels of communication should make employees equally comfortable approaching management with their interest or skills related to other duties and opportunities.

The human element of an organization is easily its most valuable and certainly the most difficult to replace. Creating and maintaining programs that uncover and leverage employees' skills and interests will result in higher workforce motivation. Employees will feel valued (and they should be valued). They will have a higher level of job satisfaction and a higher overall respect for their product, brand, and workplace.

Transportation
Transportation is a non-value-added activity. Delivery is the only form of transport for which a customer is willing to pay. Additionally, each time a product is moved, it is exposed to risks such as damage, delay, or loss, and will incur costs. Transportation is inevitably a necessary expenditure in many cases. The Lean philosophy does not prescribe that goods should stay in warehouses

to avoid transportation costs altogether, but rather advises that transportation should be minimized and identifies it as a non-value-added activity. Sensible production, focus on materials flow, and responding to the Voice of the Customer are all effective remedies to combat transportation mura.

Transportation and waiting converge in the area of facility layout and the production cycle. Many organizations could benefit from deconstructing their production method, then rebuilding it from the ground up around the product and around the needs of the customer, or even better, around a desire to be able to quickly change to meet the changing needs of the customer. The focus, however, will vary from industry to industry.

Inventory

Inventory in all forms (raw materials, work in progress, finished goods, supplies, etc.) represents income that has not been realized and, more importantly, cost. Inventory that is at any time not being actively processed is considered waste, as any other production state is a non-value-added activity (also waste).

On-hand inventory can potentially incur very high costs, and therefore many organizations are employing methods such as *small lot production*, pull production systems, and Just-in-Time inventory, all of which are discussed later in this text. The topic of inventory in regard to reduction and related costs is a popular one. An entire industry of third-party logistics providers has evolved to handle not only transport, but inventory management, warehousing and storage, and even order fulfillment and distribution center management.

In this manner, some companies choose to outsource their inventory management and the warehousing of some or all of their finished goods inventory, in addition to their distribution and delivery channels. This can be beneficial especially in the realm of Just-in-Time inventory; however, interfacing with an outside company can potentially lead to communication errors and scheduling issues if executed incorrectly.

In the instance of a company attempting to implement the Lean model, the temptation to outsource and "clear your plate" of costs and waste can be high. It is important to remember that if the third party logistics provider you choose hasn't implemented their own waste reduction program or doesn't have a clearly-established value chain, they will pass those costs back onto you or your customers. This effectively negates the waste reduction attempts. The decision to outsource should be thoroughly investigated and is covered in detail later within this text.

Motion

Motion represents wasted work in the literal sense of the word. Non-value-added motion is any wear and tear, other than what is absolutely necessary for production, on machines that produce value-added activity. This concept is also applicable to the workforce in the form of repetitive strain injuries or of productivity maximization programs.

Motion is an interesting waste to address. In many circumstances the concept of delegating repetitive or repeatable precision-focused tasks to machine or computer-integrated components instead of workforce components is a favorable option for reducing wasted human motion as well as the risk of human error. This Lean concept of waste examines the totality of the action and its role as a value-added activity regardless of by whom it is completed. In this sense, the scales are tipped by the customer's needs and the role the action or process has in fulfilling those needs, and therefore the action is evaluated without bias.

There are a variety of ways to determine levels of motion, from visual observation to electronic monitors. Non-value-added motion can be reduced through the application of continuous improvement methods and process analysis to generate new, more efficient protocols.

Excessive Production

Wasteful production occurs when more products are produced than the customer requires. Traditional manufacturing of large batches is a major culprit of excessive production, and with businesses needing to become increasingly flexible to meet changing customer and market needs, excessive production can represent large circumstances of waste or numerous waste events. In this way, excessive production is considered the most serious form of waste due to the fact that it generates waste events in other aspects of production as well.

Excessive production is linked to waste in the areas of inventory (storage and liquidation), transportation, and motion. And like defects, excessive production can cause waste through reworking or through scrap, or prevent the timely detection of defects within quality control systems. The uniform flow of materials can also be disrupted, causing other waste events in the areas of muri and mura (overburden and unevenness). With the replacement of traditional "push" production systems and a focus on smaller batch production, organizations have found manufacturing and production protocols to help reduce waste events linked to excessive production.

2. A Broad View

While the first aspect deals with the all-important process of identifying—and reducing—waste, the second component of Lean philosophy deals with strategy and planning. Lean focuses on thinking strategically and incorporating long-term planning into everyday operations. An organization's success should be viewed with a focus on the long term and in the context of the industry-at-large; short-term gains are not a reliable measure of success. This approach is not intended to trivialize short-term development, but rather to put it in perspective toward maintaining a competitive advantage within a given industry.

If, for example, a firm's goal is to acquire the lion's share of the market within which they operate, then a large variety of factors must be taken into account. If this firm's (Firm A) sales goals are consistently beaten by 9 percent each quarter, that is certainly good news. When taking a broad view, however, the firm sees that a competitor (Firm B) is consistently beating their own sales goals by 11 percent. This is still not quite the big picture and doesn't present instructive insight.

Firm B owns a smaller market share than Firm A, and though sales are on the rise, that smaller market share translates into lower overall profits. While Firm B is making aggressive sales, Firm A is still on track to *their* strategic goals. This contextualizes the rate of Firm B's growth, and can help decision makers at Firm A further realize their organization's goals.

Conceptually, the broad view approach can be implemented at the day-to-day level by matching tactical and operational tasks and decisions with strategic level goals and avoiding *tunnel vision* style production. Tunnel vision production focuses on the product or the process and not on the customer, therefore making non-value-added activities harder to detect and, in many cases, leading to excessive production.

Firm A's strategic goal was to control the largest market share in each of its businesses' product lines, but perhaps the strategic goal of Firm B was to offer superior service and quality. These broad view strategies can be reduced to their simplest terms by working backward—superior service means on-time delivery, on-time delivery means tight scheduling on the factory floor, tight scheduling means examining processes, etc. Once the day-to-day functional building blocks are established at the production level, their supervision and execution can be tied to the broad view strategy and help align business activities at all levels of the organization. The practice of aligning daily operations with a "broad view" mentality ensures that all decisions are matched appropriately to the organization's long-term goals.

This approach also helps organizations to avoid becoming too goal-focused, which at face value doesn't sound like a negative circumstance at all. But consider this: if a team or a department is too focused on simply reaching its established goals or conforming to its specified budget, then there is a significant opportunity for those individuals to lose track of the company's overall waste reduction goals. Work could be done toward goals that don't fit into the company's strategic position, creating more work, which inevitably will be non-value-added waste. Work could be done to meet a deadline "at all costs," creating waste through overburdening or production that is at high risk for defects. At all levels of the organization, goals should be uniform and each should represent the realization of another step toward long-term goals.

This process creates a "checks and balances" environment that not only keeps the organization on track with its long-term strategy but also gives front-line management a structure for decision-making. When implementing a new production schedule or examining current facility load, the decision-maker needs to compare his or her plan to the overall plan and ask the questions: *"Does this program reflect the company's desire to fulfill these criteria?"* and *"How does my plan conform to the company's waste reduction standards?"* This approach minimizes waste created by the front line having to "change gears" as their performance fluctuates from the strategic level plan. The concept of a broad view is designed not only to keep a company's operations on track, but also to reduce waste in all forms: overburden, unevenness, and wasteful production.

In conjunction with visibility, another of Lean's core philosophies, an organization that utilizes a "broad view" mentality should consider its supply chain in the context of a network instead of a number of singular buyer and supplier relationships. This inclusive context reflects the relationships that those suppliers have with suppliers of their own, and reflects the relationship an organization ultimately has with the downstream end user, even if that customer is removed from the organization by other firms.

fig. 3

Traditional Supply Chain Interpretation

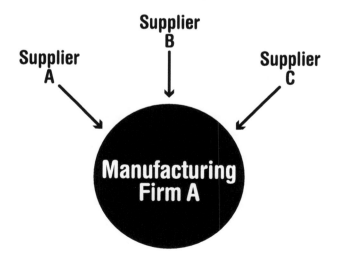

fig. 4

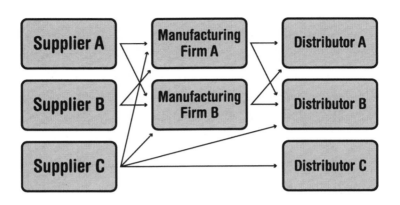

Network Supply Chain Interpretation

fig. 5

Hierarchy of Organizational Planning

3. Simplicity

Simplicity is a golden rule in many fields. If companies "reap what they sow," then simple in means simple out, and a process that produces simple is simple throughout. Simplicity reduces the human error component in many cases and can make fixing errors easier as well. Simplicity also speaks to the Lean business model's waste reduction approach. Focusing energy and resources on a complicated problem can be alleviated by reducing a complex scenario into simpler parts, and simple problems generally have simple solutions.

Simple processes are easier to teach, and they are easier to implement. Simple configurations have lower chances of producing defects or errors due to malfunctions or "moving part syndrome." Derived from the no-nonsense world of engineering, moving part syndrome is the theory that the chances of defect increase with the number of moving parts.

Simple operations are easier to monitor, and sources of waste are more easily identified. In some production applications a simple approach may mean reducing the number of processes or cycles at a specific workstation. This may create more workstations but will improve flexibility, allowing the process at each workstation to be tweaked to compensate for changing production needs or to rectify defective production.

Another aspect of Lean's simplistic approach is apparent in what creating an effective *value stream* strives to do in the first place: differentiate between value-added and non-value-added activities. This is certainly not necessarily a simple task, but with the narrowing of focus comes a lessening of clutter and mixed signals. It is in this spirit that Lean focuses not on departments and their functions but on the processes themselves that create the products and value for the customer. If the process is established as the most important aspect of production, then the departments will be restructured as needed or tasked accordingly to match the flow of value-added activities. Simplicity also reduces wasteful motion. If every activity and task at a workstation is as simple and productive as necessary, there is less room for unneeded motion.

4. Continuous Improvement

The kaizen culture built around continuous improvement affects a company in the most positive way possible. This concept makes for an "easier said than done" situation, but it is essential for contemporary firms to maintain their competitive edge. In addition to all of the merits that have already been touched on about the core of kaizen, a culture of continuous improvement also creates a corporate environment that is receptive to change. This is essential in the contemporary marketplace and is an asset for any organization.

Change can come from a multitude of sources, changing customer needs, market fluctuations, natural disasters, threats from competition, and regional attitudes being just a few examples. Companies that don't change get left behind, and a company with a healthy attitude toward change can maintain a flexible position within its industry, which is another core component of the Lean philosophy.

The concept of continuous improvement is not only enabled by staff at all levels but by company policy and practices. Many of the Lean components reflect the foundation that an organization requires to tirelessly self-improve—specifically a drive for simplicity and visibility, but also the focus on waste elimination and employee contribution. A strong appreciation for employees and their efforts at improvement will help to generate goodwill toward the company at the very least, and at the most will push the organization to new heights through the most effective utilization of its employees. The original Toyota Production System innovation arose from time spent dedicated to kaizen activities. These activities reflected brainstorming, process observation, and mandatory improvement suggestions from all levels of staff.

In implementation, the kaizen system represents a cycle. Continuous improvement is not a one-time activity but the product of ongoing efforts. This cycle of process examination is also referred to as ***PDCA*** (Plan, Do, Check, Adjust), the Deming cycle, or the Shewhart cycle. In each iteration of the process, the specific components are implemented with slight variation, but the objective and method remain the same. These programs represent cyclic processes that strive for continuous improvement and provide a template for achievement. Within the Toyota Production System, kaizen activity can be represented as a series of steps that work in conjunction with PDCA.

- Set operations and activities to a uniform standard
- Measure operations and activities to establish a benchmark
- Compare benchmarks to requirements or goals
- Increase productivity and reduce waste though innovation
- Re-measure to establish a new benchmark and verify successful progress
- Restart the cycle with the newly standardized operations

PDCA

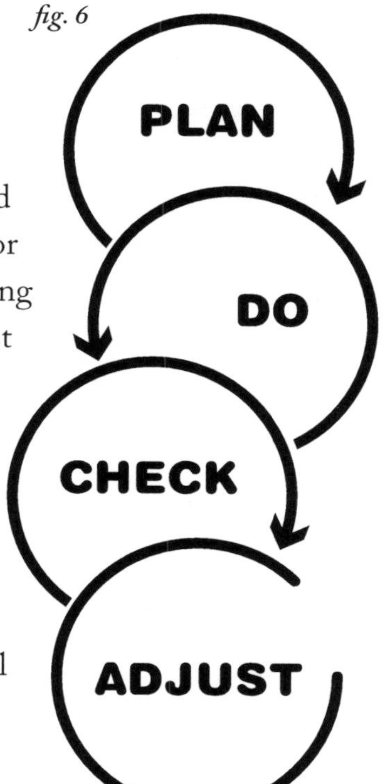

PDCA follows the same concept of product and process control as well as continuous improvement. Planning encompasses establishing objectives and methods for reaching those objectives or goals. If the changes needed are sweeping or far-reaching, it can be prudent to test methodology on a smaller scale or in circumstances in which the consequences can be tracked or mitigated as needed. The "do" portion is the execution of the plan. Data collection at this stage is necessary for the next two stages and to measure goal achievement throughout.

fig. 6

PLAN

DO

CHECK

ADJUST

Checking uses the data collected from the previous step compared against the results and, more importantly, the goals established in the initial planning stage. Here variation from the plan should be identified as well as any differences. Variation is important in two ways. Primarily, variation can be deviation that falls short of established goals (failure), but it can also have unexpected positive consequences. While these outcomes were neither planned for nor identified from the outset, variation that generates positive outcomes should be identified and logged for use in the next step. Keeping an open mind when conducting performance evaluations such as the PDCA process is important and helps ensure that no solution is left "on the table." An open mind and a willingness to listen to brainstorm-style ideas is a necessity with the implementation of kaizen-style continuous improvement. The final adjustment stage is the implementation of corrective action. Corrective action should be implemented only after the sources of negative variation can be identified to avoid wasteful action, and all corrective action should be precise and targeted specifically to work in tandem with goal achievement.

But what if the PDCA process doesn't produce innovation?

In an instance in which the PDCA process produces no variation and no room for improvement, the scope of the process can be scaled down to reduce components to their constituents. Decision makers should consider narrowing the focus of PDCA efforts. Or a dead end PDCA improvement process can be re-targeted to examine the problem from another angle. If that doesn't work either, perhaps the barrier lies at the workstation before, after, or within an unexpected aspect of production. Covered later in this text, Ishikawa diagrams (aka fishbone diagrams) are effective cause-and-effect maps that get to the source of the problem and direct improvement efforts.

A3 Problem Solving
A practical adaptation of the PDCA process cycle is the A3 approach to problem solving. *A3 problem solving*—also known as

Systematic Problem Solving (SPS)—is a structured approach that uses a single ISO A3 (11"x17" size) sheet of paper to employ eight prescribed problem-solving steps. While the number of steps can vary, the following detail covers a basic outline for the A3 method.

1. Initial Perceptions

This is a description of the problem to serve as a background for the problem-solving effort at hand. Framed as a business case, the background incorporates details such as strategic impact, financial impact, impact across the organization, supply chain impact (both upstream and down), and any other pertinent details.

While quantitative data may be useful at this stage, information that is selected should primarily be qualitative.

2. Breakdown of the Problem

This is a statement that consists of identifying the causes and specifics of the problem. This could be through structured analysis using something like the 5W1H method (covered later in this text) or any other structured investigative method.

This step is defined as an actionable clarification of the problem, and it should include more quantitative than qualitative data.

3. Target Setting

Establishing well-defined goals that seek to remedy the problem detailed in the last step is the purpose of the target setting stage. Firm goals—goals based on both qualitative and quantitative data. The overall purpose of this stage is to determine what this undertaking is attempting to accomplish.

It is important to note that the fewer targets that are set at this stage the better. The purpose of the A3 problem-solving method is to narrow the focus of efforts while simultaneously completely scouring out the root of a problem. As is often stated, this is a common theme in Lean implementation and is in line with the overriding concept of kaizen and waste reduction: continuous incremental improvement and the replacement of inefficiency (non-value-added) with efficiency (value-added).

4. Root Cause Analysis

This is the thorough exploration of the most basic causes of the problem. By building on earlier investigations and using tools such as the Ishikawa (fishbone) diagram, the root causes of the problem are discovered and recorded.

Depending on the complexity of the problem, this stage may vary in duration and effort. If the scope of a problem is found to be systemic, or too large in scope to be accurately summarized using a sheet of A3-sized paper, then not only is the focus too wide to employ this method, but other, more drastic, measures should be taken.

5. Corrective Actions

Based on the root causes of the problem at hand determined in the last step, countermeasures are devised to do the following:

    a. correct the root cause and remedy the problem

    b. maintain a focus on the established goals and aim for the targets that have been set

This step should consist of a detailed plan that prescribes targeted action. Corrective action plans should specify resources to be allocated and the people who will participate in deployment and execution.

6. Confirmation of Effect

Once the corrective measures have been implemented, monitor the results. Were your efforts successful? Did this program correctly ascertain the root causes of the problem at hand and reduce the impacts stated in the business case outlined within the first stage?

The results of this stage are critical in determining what the follow-up action will be.

7. Follow-Up Action

This is the appropriate action to be taken once the effect of the countermeasures has been determined. If the problem has been successfully eliminated, then the communication of your success is in order. Termed "lateral deployment of findings to other groups"[1] this follow-up action is critical to waste reduction and the sustainment of gains. Once rolled out across the organization, this new standard of efficient operation becomes the benchmark for continued growth.

There is no communication of success *without* success, however, so the report of findings cannot be made without also sustaining the achievement of the goals established within the target-setting stage. In true form to the PDCA system, each of the A3 activities is better described as a process, and the problem solving system is cyclic as a result.

---

[1] In Japanese, the concept of lateral findings deployment is called *yoko-narabi-tenkai*.

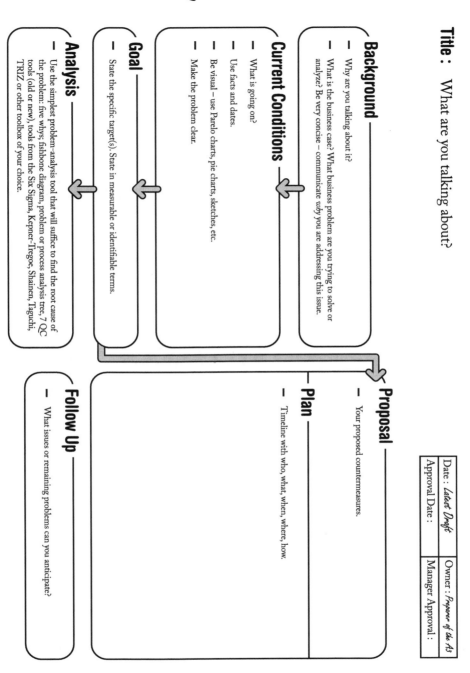

Title : What are you talking about?

Background

— Why are you talking about it?

— What is the business case? What business problem are you trying to solve or analyze? Be very concise – communicate *why* you are addressing this issue.

Current Conditions

— What is going on?

— Use facts and dates.

— Be visual – use Parelo charts, pie charts, sketches, etc.

— Make the problem clear.

Goal

— State the specific target(s). State in measurable or identifiable terms.

Analysis

— Use the simplest problem-analysis tool that will suffice to find the root cause of the problem: five whys; fishbone diagram, problem or process analysis tree, 7 QC tools (old or new), tools from the Six Sigma, Kepner-Tregoe, Shainen, Taguchi, TRIZ or other toolbox of your choice.

Proposal

— Your proposed countermeasures.

Plan

— Timeline with who, what, when, where, how.

Follow Up

— What issues or remaining problems can you anticipate?

| Date : *Latest Draft* | Owner : *Preparer of the A3* |
| Approval Date : | Manager Approval : |

fig. 7 : A sample A3 master sheet. Note that the terminology within each of the steps can vary, though the intent remains the same.

This means that a failure to achieve goals means going back through the process and determining what additional corrective action is necessary. This may mean further investigation into the root causes of the problem. It may mean a narrower focus, or selecting and mapping alternative countermeasures.

plan

1. Initial Perceptions
- A description of the problem
- Framed as a business case

2. Breakdown of the Problem
- Uses structured analysis
- Clarification of the problem

3. Target Setting
- Establishes goals
- Uses quantitative data

4. Root Cause Analysis
- Identification of the problem's root causes
- Ishikawa or fishbone diagrams

do

5. Corrective Actions
- Mapped countermeasures to reduce the problem and meet goals
- Detailed plan

check

6. Confirmation of Effect
- What was the result of the corrective efforts?
- Was the problem solved or does it persist?

act

7. Follow-Up Action
- Share findings across the organization
- Return to the planning stages if countermeasures were unsuccessful

fig. 8: The A3 problem-solving method framed as an extension of the PDCA cycle. Note how each of the A3 steps can be classified as corresponding to a portion of the PDCA method.

5. Visibility

Visibility within an organization and within an organization's supply chain is much more than organizational transparency. Waste can only be eliminated if it can be identified, and invisible waste will go on unchecked indefinitely. In short, visibility leads to action. This philosophy permeates all levels of operation, from the CEO's desk all the way down to the mail room. In a practical, operational implementation, facilities should be open and uncluttered. Software systems should likewise be clean and uncluttered. Company correspondence and communication channels should never be chaotic or garbled.

The free sharing of information between departments prevents crossed signals and provides more opportunities for problems to be spotted. It also promotes efficiency and reduces the waste of overproduction or double work. Cluttered work environments can foster stress and confusion, as well as disrespect for the workplace. It may sound like synergy mumbo jumbo, but creating a culture of visibility among your workforce means a better work environment and a foundational stepping-stone toward a culture of continuous improvement and organizational longevity.

While each of the six Lean philosophies is integral to overall success, visibility is unique in its enabling capacity. In a visible supply chain, waste is easily identified and therefore eliminated. If operations are transparent to all members of the workforce, operator and employee input can produce simplified processes based on a total experience greater than the sum of its parts.

As a practice, visibility also ensures that the organization is maintaining a broad view stance through careful matching of operations to long-term strategy and by the exposure of tasks that do not add value or do not match corporate goals. Additionally, staff alignment with goals and operational objectives leads to faster responses to changing conditions without losing sight of set targets. This enables a flexible response to changing market conditions and allows for a smoother transition. The smoother the transition, the lower the chance of creating waste during the change. A high degree of visibility means that the organization will have more information and an earlier warning that change is necessary. In situations in which staying the course means hitting an iceberg, an early warning can mean successful navigation to safer waters.

Visibility also works with a broad view mentality in the supply chain, both upstream and down. When viewing a supply chain as a network, a level of dynamic transparency is needed to ensure that goods and materials flow appropriately and without waste. However, this can be difficult, depending on the relationships a firm has with its suppliers and customers. In some supply networks, complete integration of systems exists so that suppliers can generate orders automatically based on real-time visibility of the buyer's inventory of raw materials. This is obviously a very advanced and very beneficial relationship to both parties, but levels of visibility and cooperation should be present within all buyer and supplier networks to ensure a productive relationship for both parties.

The focus on visibility is not exclusive to Lean. Stepping outside the frame of Lean for a moment and examining "best practices" for conventional businesses in all fields and industries, we see the importance of visibility in the supply chain. This is a crucial component of successful business operations and logistics for maintaining a competitive advantage. The establishment of a high-visibility supply chain is an important platform to develop and implement Lean. In order for a company to maintain its competitive edge, it is crucial that each department or facet of the company that is engaged in value-added processes contributes to the information flow.

Poor communication can result in cost for any company and is a root cause, in some form, of all of the sources of waste. Poor communication also causes distortion within the supply chain, and, in addition to causing numerous waste events, it can affect perception of brand and quality. If distortion occurs in regard to customer needs, then what the company delivers could be radically different from what the customer expected, which is the exact opposite of a customer service focus. If too little information is shared about common goals and the company's overriding goals, then departments may default to a "profit maximizing" mode in which department heads focus only on results for their own portion of the value-added process. This may sound like a productive approach at first, but the fact of the matter is, this tunnel-vision approach usually means that other departments suffer while one posts record productivity and profit. If the focus is instead placed on the production cycle as a process and on value-added activities, then departments or business units are not incentivized to deviate from the company's production protocols and standards.

Visibility and information sharing must occur to ensure all departments are in line with the company's short- and long-term goals, as well as to ensure departmental cooperation and success as a team. In short, visibility is the key to making a company more than the sum of its parts.

6. Flexibility

Flexibility is an essential characteristic in the business world, because market conditions and customer needs are constantly changing. Additionally, flexibility and continuous improvement go hand in hand in making employees and overall corporate culture tolerant of and even hungry for change. The phrase "change is inevitable" can now be extended in the business world to say "change is inevitable for survival." A company that is ready to change is more prepared to succeed in the current business climate.

A focus on flexibility also means less friction when dealing with changing customer needs. While not listed as a source of waste, resistance to the needs of the customer can result in intangibly damaging waste events in the areas of reputation or service. Additionally, new ideas regarding the reduction of waste can require radically different programs whose implementation can create higher efficiency processes. A firm that's ready to move to the next level will see smoother transitions when adopting new programs and practices, meaning reductions in downtime, both literally and in D.O.W.N.T.I.M.E. waste reduction.

fig. 9

The Six Components of Lean Philosophy

1. Continual Elimination of Waste

- Identify the eight sources of waste
- Differentiate between value-added and non-value-added activities

2. Goals with a Broad View

- Goals drive tasks
- Tasks are matched with organizational objectives at all levels

3. Simplicity

- Simpler solutions are better solutions
- Complex problems exist as simpler, smaller problems

4. Continuous Improvement

- Learning from the past is growth
- Understand how all six philosophies are related and interdependent
- Understand that what you build today is the foundation for tomorrow

5. Organizational Visibility

- Visible problems are solvable; invisible problems are not
- Visibility at all levels encourages continuous improvement

6. Flexibility

- The organization must be ready to respond to a changing market environment
- The organization must be ready to respond to changing customer needs
- The organization must be prepared to restructure to survive

Chapter Review

The Lean production method strives to differentiate between value-added and non-value-added activities (waste). Waste can be categorized into three overarching categories: physical waste, unevenness of flow, and overburden. Further narrowed, the sources of physical waste can be categorized into one or more of the following types of waste events: defective production, overprocessing, waiting, under-utilized (non-used) employee talent, transportation, inventory, motion, and excessive production. Together, these sources form the acronym D.O.W.N.T.I.M.E.

In addition to vigilant waste reduction activities, the Lean philosophy prescribes five other pillars: the concept of having a broad view, or focusing on the wide-reaching impacts of strategic decisions; the concept of constant simplification to reduce "moving parts syndrome"; the culture of kaizen, or of continuous improvement and innovation from all levels of the organization; the concept that visibility reduces effort and leads to action; and the idea that a flexible position provides and sustains an unbeatable competitive edge.

Problem solving tools that have a wide application across the Lean methodology and beyond are the PDCA cycle, a Plan-Do-Check-Act continual feedback process that builds a simple and structured approach to improving processes. A practical application of this method is the A3 problem solving approach. A3 problem solving narrows the focus of investigative efforts and standardizes the improvement process.

To Recap

- The Lean production method strives to differentiate between value-added and non-value-added activities (waste).

- Waste can be categorized into three overarching categories: physical waste, unevenness of flow, and overburden. Further narrowed, the sources of physical waste can be categorized into one or more of the following types of waste events: defective production, overprocessing, waiting, under-utilized (non-used) employee talent, transportation, inventory, motion, and excessive production. Together, these sources form the acronym D.O.W.N.T.I.M.E.

- In addition to vigilant waste reduction activities, the Lean philosophy prescribes five other pillars: the concept of having a broad view, or focusing on the wide-reaching impacts of strategic decisions; the concept of constant simplification to reduce "moving parts syndrome"; the culture of kaizen, or of continuous improvement and innovation from all levels of the organization; the concept that visibility reduces effort and leads to action; and the idea that a flexible position provides and sustains an unbeatable competitive edge.

- A problem solving tool with a wide application across the Lean methodology and beyond is the PDCA cycle, a Plan-Do-Check-Act continual feedback process that builds a simple and structured approach to improving processes. A practical application of this method is the A3 problem solving approach. A3 problem solving narrows the focus of investigative efforts and standardizes the improvement process.

1. The Lean philosophy of manufacturing and production seeks to differentiate value-added activities from those that do not add value. Non-value-added activities are also known as what?

   a) effort   b) production
   c) quality   d) waste

2. The concept of kaizen permeates the entire Lean model. Kaizen is a focus on what business activity?

   a) financial accountability   b) continuous improvement
   c) customer relations   d) maximum productive effort

3. Which of the following is not one of the core components of Lean philosophy?

   a) visibility   b) accountability
   c) a broad view   d) flexibility

4. An organization that employs the Lean methodology understands that innovation comes exclusively from management and research and development endeavors.

   a) true   b) false

5. The PDCA process is which one of the following types of tools?

   a) process improvement tool   b) staff development tool
   c) manufacturing tool   d) PDCA is not a tool

| 2 |

Lean Production

In This Chapter

- The core of Lean manufacturing, the pull production system, is explored in detail
- Value stream mapping is discussed
- Organization, scheduling, and efficiency tools such as kanban, Just-in-Time, and Single Minute Exchange of Die are all explained as tools within the context of Lean
- Facility layout configurations and other companion tools to the Lean system, such as production leveling, are examined

While the first chapter of this book started off with the building blocks of the Lean method—its philosophy and guiding principles—this chapter focuses on the nuts and bolts processes that comprise production within the Lean framework. While many of these methods can be used outside of the Lean model, they work best in concert with one another and in line with Lean's guiding principles of continuous improvement, flexibility, and waste reduction.

The Pull Production System

Organizational supply chains have traditionally been focused on forecasting demand using a variety of statistical models and gathered data, then producing ample goods to meet the anticipated needs. In this method the anticipation of demand "pushes" the production of goods through the supply chain, for which the batch required would generate the order for the raw materials required.

This demand can be classified as artificial; there is no concrete indication that there are customers who have a utility or desire for the goods entering production. Due to the artificial nature of this demand, the levels of goods that are produced can vary wildly from actual demand.

Under the push method of production, when raw materials enter the production cycle, the next manufacturing process is applied and the goods move on to the next, and so on until they are finished. In many cases manufacturers employing the push production system also produce surplus goods as a buffer against shipping delays, damage, and loss or to insulate their anticipated (artificial) demand from fluctuation. Of course this method of production violates many of the waste reduction components of Lean, often creating waiting queues, excessive production, high inventory levels, and unnecessary transport.

Lean manufacturing is based on the "pull" production system, where customer demand "pulls" production through the supply chain. In practice, this means that the final steps of the production process determine the levels of production of each station before it. The result, as opposed to the push method, is customer requests for goods creating orders for raw materials that work backward—backward compared to the push method—through the production process.

In a traditional system, raw materials would be fed through each process with each workstation producing a more finished product based on the pieces sent to it. By contrast, in a *pull production system*, each workstation requests, from the stage before it, only the materials or components needed to perform its process. If there is no need for a particular material or component, no request is made, and in this way excessive levels of inventory are prevented, along with reductions in all areas of waste, such as motion, wait times, transportation, and overprocessing.

When the final stages of production and the needs of the customer are the focus of the pull production system, companies can tailor their production lines to fit demand in real time. Goods are produced as needed in realistic batch sizes, and ***buffer inventory*** is greatly reduced along with on-hand inventory.

fig. 10   **The Pull Production System**

But if the pull production system is so much better, and is such an obvious solution to systemic production challenges, why did it only just come about with the Toyota Production System? To answer that, we have to take a deeper look into why the ***push production system*** is so widely used, and in what ways the pull production system uses innovation to overcome production challenges.

Push production relies on ***economies of scale***, or the method of spreading out costs over a larger number of parts produced, specifically fixed costs. If a part costs five dollars to produce at a rate of 10,000 units per week, with three dollars of that five dedicated to fixed costs and two dollars dedicated to variable costs, then economies of scale tell decision makers to simply make more parts to reduce the three-dollar portion of the equation.

Variable costs are often tied to the volume of production. They include aspects such as the cost of raw materials—more units mean more materials consumed, but because units are mass-produced the amount of material consumed by each should be the same—and other intermittent costs such as labor and the rate of degradation to equipment and consumables. Fixed costs are often tied to long-lived assets, which accountants refer to as PPE: property, plant, and equipment. These costs include equipment, utilities, and the cost of line changes.

By ramping up the number of units—otherwise known as increasing batch size—between line changes, that three dollars' worth of fixed costs from our example above could be squeezed down to one dollar per unit if the rate of production was tripled. Calculating the rate at which variable costs increase is a bit more complicated than simply dividing the cost by the number of units, and the particulars of that calculation are outside the scope of this text; however, experienced production managers would scale production so that the increase in variable cost did not offset the savings gained through leveraging the economies of scale and reducing fixed costs.

This additional production creates a savings in one area while incurring potentially massive cost in another. Because line changes can be so expensive, large batches are utilized to spread costs out, though in many cases savings are chipped away by the costs of carrying additional inventory further down the supply chain. This is clearly oppositional to Lean's focus on waste reduction through nearly every aspect of D.O.W.N.T.I.M.E. waste, and it also ignores the voice of the customer through reliance on artificial demand.

The pull production system, on the other hand, relies on small batch sizes, quick line changes, and other innovative methods detailed within this chapter to completely change the way flexible manufacturing is implemented: in a way that focuses on the needs of the customer (actual demand).

Alone, no component of the pull production system would change traditional push methods into the efficient and productive Lean configuration; only when employed simultaneously do all the pieces of the pull production system fall into place.

Value Stream Mapping

Value stream mapping is a Lean management tool used to analyze the current state of all activities and processes of a product or service, from absolute beginning all the way through to the end user (customer). This tool is also used to design new processes and methods and can be a valuable asset in identifying waste and differentiating it from value-added activities. The goal of effective value stream mapping is to identify opportunities for improvement in the areas of cost, waste, and efficiency.

Value stream mapping takes an approach different from the traditional more linear and isolated view of production and its supporting processes. While no production organization ever thought of production as existing in a vacuum, value stream mapping takes the interdependent interpretation to a whole new level. It is this understanding of the web of inputs creating value, as opposed to a more linear concept of production, that gives decision makers a more comprehensive overview of their production operations.

Value stream mapping is not only a foundational element of understanding production, but of implementing the pull production system and of making real progress with kaizen-related activities. Once processes are mapped, a baseline or benchmark is established. Then, future improvement efforts and kaizen activities can be measured against the system's current state.

Implementation requires identification of a particular product line, product family, or service. The program and goals are then outlined along with known issues. The best mapping is done on the production floor or during the execution of production activities. This means that the data gathered is as true to life as possible and that the value stream is not distorted (remember, visibility reduces distortion and improves waste identification). Important elements to include are current steps, delays or waiting queues, information flows, and flows of materials. Value stream mapping is not exclusive to manufacturing and production. The process being mapped could be the production of finished goods—raw materials to the delivery of finished goods. In a wider application it could be a design flow process—the concept-to-launch process. Value stream mapping is also applicable for service supply chains in the sense that they could track all of the activities done in preparation for the execution of the service. This could include supplies, equipment preparation, space preparation, or creation of the service environment or atmosphere.

After the stream is mapped, an assessment process should begin to identify waste, inefficiency, and opportunity for improvement. Information for these decisions comes from the methods outlined in the toolbox below, as well as observation and data gathering. As these areas are noted, plans should be drawn for a new value stream map that takes into account the modifications to the current system of processes. These new conditions should represent achievement of the waste reduction and efficiency goals initially set forth with the start of the value stream mapping process and should, like all constructive goals, be realistic, achievable, and sustainable.

As with any improvement program, performance and goal realization need to be checked to verify achievement. These *lag measures* are a follow-up to the design and implementation of a new value stream map that has been modified to meet the goals for efficiency improvement and waste reduction. Like all aspects of continuous improvement, improvement through value stream mapping is a cycle; once it has been implemented, the next step is to begin the process again.

fig. 11

Value Stream Mapping

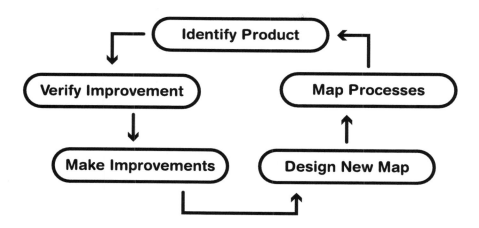

Value Stream Mapping Toolbox

Value stream mapping as a process is not entirely free-form. There is an established set of tools for a firm's management seeking to implement value stream mapping.

The toolbox consists of the following seven components:

1. Process Activity Mapping
2. Supply Chain Responsiveness Matrix
3. Production Variety Funnel
4. Quality Filter Mapping
5. Demand Amplification Mapping
6. Decision Point Analysis
7. Physical Structure Mapping

Process Activity Mapping

Process activity mapping is a value stream tool that has its origins in industrial engineering. It is a narrower method of determining the components of the entire value stream and is similar in design to the program of value stream mapping. Unlike the large-scale overview that value stream mapping presents, process activity mapping focuses on a single process or set of processes. Process activity mapping can be a useful tool when building a comprehensive value stream map, as well as taking a deeper dive into a single process or business activity.

This process is implemented in the following steps:

1. Select and study a specific process
2. Identify areas in which waste occurs
3. Determine if the process can be reconfigured and produce the same outcome
4. Determine if the flow pattern will improve with reconfiguration
5. Determine if all associated tasks are strictly value-added and necessary

An observational and quantitative data collection is made of the process. The result is a process map, showing the flow of materials and all value-added activities. Recordings of machine cycles, motion of people and machines, distance moved, and time taken are used to calculate totals in each category. A process activity map can serve as a model for future improvement efforts and can highlight areas of non-value-added activity. An example of a popular technique for determining the characteristics of a task is the *5W1H* analysis shown below. It answers the questions why, who, what, where, when, and how.

fig. 12

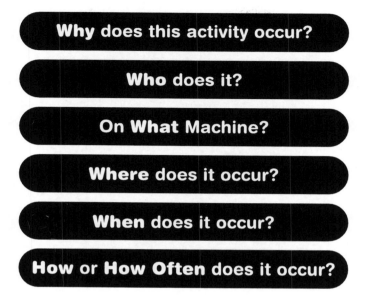

Why does this activity occur?

Who does it?

On What Machine?

Where does it occur?

When does it occur?

How or How Often does it occur?

The goal of this process is to eliminate activities that are redundant or unnecessary. It also seeks to simplify or combine other activities and produce changes that will reduce waste. As with all value chain mapping, various models may be explored before selecting the final solution.

Supply Chain Responsiveness Matrix

This visual tool is an analysis of an organization's lead time and inventory levels. The matrix is constructed by graphing lead time along the x-axis and inventory levels along the y-axis. The resulting graph shows where slow-moving stock is located. The final product demonstrates the time constraints for a particular process, and once underperforming areas are identified, corrective action can be implemented.

Production Variety Funnel

This value stream mapping tool is designed to identify to which set of internal operations models a manufacturing firm conforms. Each model has a different set of characteristics that are fairly uniform across different organizations, and effective determination of the appropriate designation can assist with forecasting and production scheduling. It can also provide planners with a comprehensive graph of how the supply chain network and the firm operate and how complexities must be managed. This method is also referred to as an ***IVAT analysis***, an acronym referring to the different designations of production. In this instance, the letters that form the acronym represent the physical shape of the production process as outlined below, not the first letter of their respective names.

- "I" production consists of the manufacture of many identical items with few variations. This is a typical configuration for many consumer goods and commodities.

- "V" configurations consist of a wide array of finished products produced from a small number of raw materials. This configuration is common in the textiles industry, or in many service industries such as restaurants.

- "A" configured production is the opposite of "V." It is a narrow assortment of finished goods produced from a large number of varying raw materials. This configuration normally has several different value streams and can utilize multiple facilities for production. An example of "A" production would be assembly manufacturing, or the type of manufacturing most closely associated with complex machinery or automobiles.

- "T" production configurations use various combinations of products made from specific components. The components are produced into semi-processed parts that are held for commitment to final versions as demanded by customers. The household appliance industry is an example of "T" configuration processing; there may be a thousand washing machines produced, but only two hundred of them will be equipped with premium features. The number of premium units could be the result of artificial push demand or actual customer demand. The tool that is used to determine where and how this demand impacts the production process is known as a ***decision point analysis***, and is covered later in this segment.

Because production conforms to one of the IVAT configurations, this tool can be used not only to research how a supply chain will react to different hypothetical conditions, but IVAT analysis can also direct targeted inventory reduction methods.

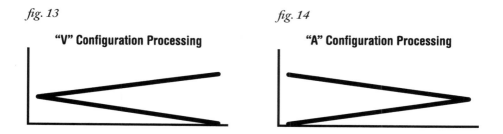

fig. 13

"V" Configuration Processing

fig. 14

"A" Configuration Processing

Quality Filter Mapping

Quality filter mapping is used as a visual representation of where quality issues exist within an organization or a value stream. This tool is used to identify three types of quality-related issues: product defects, service defects, and internal scrap.

Product defects represent defective production of finished goods that is not identified by quality control inspection. These defects are discovered by the customer and, like all quality issues, affect the perception of an organization as one that does or does not produce quality products. Service defects are quality issues not related to the finished goods themselves. These could include early or late delivery, orders that are incorrect or incomplete, or lost paperwork. Internal scrap is defective production that is caught by quality control inspection, and includes the costs of reworking if necessary, or the possible salvaging of defective production.

fig. 15

Quality Filter Mapping

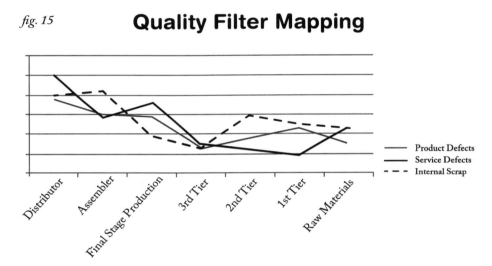

The above graphic is an example of a thorough quality filter map. Viewed without context, this chart only tells decision makers the stages in the production process where defects and related costs spike, but considering the Lean focus on visibility and waste reduction, a quality filter map can become a valuable tool to uncover sources of waste and consistently poor quality. For example, the spike in service-related defects during the final stage production phase indicate that something is wrong or is creating waste, but that it isn't machine or production related.

This "visibility leads to action" mindset is a common thread of the Lean method, and would direct decision makers to investigate non-machine-related issues within the final stage production phase. This could be done through simple observation or the more structured process activity mapping tool.

The bottom line is that when directed by a comprehensive quality filter map, decision makers and production problem solvers can hone in on areas of concern with a much more guided focus.

Demand Amplification Mapping

Also known as *Forrester Effect Mapping*, *Demand Amplification Mapping* is a method of identifying production needs for demand within specific time intervals. Forrester's research showed that as demand moved from inventory to inventory within a supply chain, the amplification or distortion of that demand would occur with each transfer. Distorted demand can generate excess levels of inventory, excessive production, waiting, motion, and transport. All of these waste events contribute negatively to a uniform flow of materials through the production process and through the supply chain.

In practice, demand amplification mapping is a graph plotted with two curves. The first curve is actual demand. This could be point-of-sale data, sales records, or shipping records, the obtaining of which is easier if there is a high degree of transparency between members of a supply chain network. The second curve is orders placed by the supplier to meet actual demand. The resulting graph is a tool to determine value stream configuration as well as to manage or reduce fluctuation, and it can even be extended to map up or downstream within a supply chain network.

Understanding demand at the root—actual demand as opposed to artificial demand—is a key component of cutting through demand amplification. When a manufacturer and a retailer or dealer have a close relationship, POS (point-of-sale) data can be helpful in establishing hard numbers to gauge demand. Additionally, a highly developed supply chain that uses Just-in-Time techniques and kanban-style replenishment can coordinate together to reduce the effects of demand amplification.

fig. 16

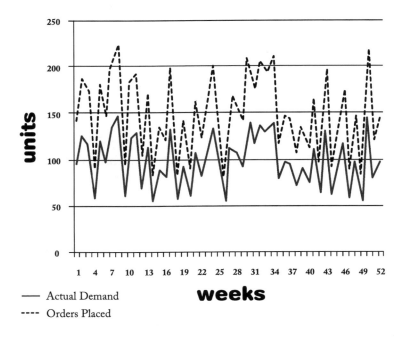

Demand Amplification Mapping

What decision makers can learn from the graphing of the Forrester Effect is the disparity between actual demand and artificial demand that was not the product of incorrect pull production, but a communication failure. Visibility leads to action, and if this potential source of waste is not tracked and addressed, it can quickly spiral out of control.

Decision Point Analysis

The decision point analysis tool is used primarily by production firms using the "T" configuration production scheme, but it can apply to other production models as well. The analysis is designed to identify the decision point, or the point in the supply chain at which customer pull demand gives way to demand that has been forecasted. The decision point is useful in the sense that assessing the processes upstream and downstream from that point can identify and reduce waste as well as ensure that current production processes are in line with both organizational goals and customer needs. In addition, with an established decision point, organizational planners can test hypothetical changes to the system without disturbing production. These "what if" scenarios act as models for new systems and can test innovation programs.

Ideally, a Lean organization wouldn't rely on the potentially waste-generating effects of artificial demand, but the "T" configuration of production is susceptible to "push creep." Push creep is a condition where, in anticipation of fluctuating demand, decision makers err on the side of overproduction and in turn rely on *safety stock* to compensate.

Tracking how production responds to demand, and at what point of the production process pull gives way to push demand, can mark areas where potential waste can occur. This value stream mapping tool is particularly useful in establishing a benchmark for production leveling activities, a topic discussed later in this chapter.

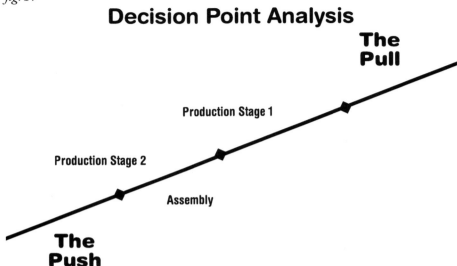

Physical Structure Mapping

Physical structure mapping is a visual representation of the structure of an entire supply chain. This process is designed to provide an overview or "bird's eye" view of a supply chain network and can be constructed in two ways. The first is a volume-based structural map. This method is effective for identifying bottlenecks and non-uniform flow—the shape of the map is directly related to the volume of production that passes through each element of the supply chain and value stream. The second method of construction is a physical structure based on cost, where the shape of each of the map's components is relative to its impact on overall cost. This model is a direct visual representation of cost centers throughout a supply chain.

Cost-Based Physical Structure Map

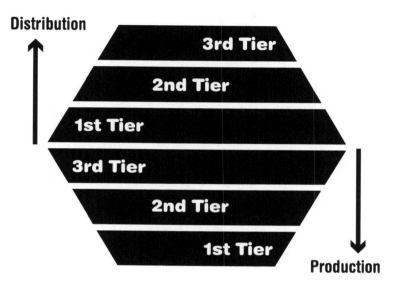

fig. 18: A physical structure map based on cost. Here, the 1st tier of distribution and the 3rd tier of production have the largest impact on costs and therefore are the primary candidates for waste reduction activities. 1st tier production and 3rd tier distribution are lower cost centers. This is representative of production that has intensive finishing work (3rd tier production) and uses outsourced distribution—the diminishing cost of distribution.

Taken individually, each of the tools in the value stream mapping toolkit provide valuable insight into operations and production activities. When used together, they are powerful investigative tools to support the value stream mapping process. For a sample value stream map and a step-by-step guide see the example on pg. 129.

Kanban

Kanban, translated from Japanese as "signboard" or "billboard," is a scheduling method for Lean manufacturing and Just-in-Time inventory (covered in detail later in this chapter). Used to control the supply chain and inventory together, kanban scheduling is designed with a whole-system focus and is conducive to improvement. Using the rate of demand to inform production, kanban scheduling is an expression of the pull production system.

Kanban methods are derived from the shelf-stocking techniques of supermarkets. When a customer removes an item from the shelf, the store's staff replenishes the sale by replacing the removed item. If a customer removes seven items, and then another removes three, the stock staff replaces ten items on the shelf. While these humble roots are just common sense, it was a revolutionary concept to implement this application on the factory floor.

The kanban method aligns inventory levels with consumption via the pull of demand. When units of material are consumed, a signal is generated to the supplier that instructs the production and delivery of the quantity needed. These signals are tracked and made visible to all parties within the supply chain for purposes of efficiency, and the result is a very flexible and adaptive supply chain. Even in environments where demand can be difficult to forecast, the travel time through the supply chain for kanban signals is so short and so well coordinated that only truly massive spikes in demand will cause disruptions.

In order for a kanban program to be effective, there are six prescribed rules that must be continuously applied and monitored. If these parameters are not consistently met, the advantages produced through the kanban system are negated in many cases, and the very system used to generate efficiency can instead produce waste events.

The six kanban rules are as follows:

1. **All later processes must start with the same number of units as earlier processes, as specified in the kanban signal.**
The integrity of the kanban system relies on the fact that only the materials needed for demand (and therefore replenishment) move through production. This means that additional materials aren't

added unnecessarily in the transit from workstation to workstation, or, along the same lines, that materials aren't deducted. This is a failsafe measure designed to ensure that 100 percent of needed materials are replenished; if materials are needed but unrecorded, then they will go without replenishment. This is an example of the opposite of visibility leading to action: invisibility leading to inaction.

2. **All earlier processes must produce the same number of units as specified in the kanban signal both in quantity and sequence.**

The kanban signal is the expression of demand and therefore the parameter by which material is pulled through production. This is a continuation of the failsafe included in the first kanban rule. Just like no unrecorded materials can enter the production process, only the requisite number of units should travel from workstation to workstation. This rule effectively creates an artificial constraint on production to prevent waste events in the form of excessive production, or on the other side of the coin, insufficient production.

3. **No items are to be made or transported without a kanban signal.**

This prohibitory constraint ensures that there are not waste events generated through the unnecessary transport of materials or their accidental introduction into production without corresponding demand. Without being called for by a kanban signal, there is no demand for units of material or goods and therefore no value to be added through their transport or production.

4. **All goods that have been called for via a kanban signal must have an attached kanban card.**

Kanban cards are covered in the next section. Suffice it to say that this parameter is a visibility and communication effort to ensure that goods are not lost or transported unnecessarily.

5. **Under no circumstances should defective goods be attached to a kanban.**
Defective production is non-value-added activity, and customers will not accept defective goods.

6. **A reduction in the number of kanban within a production system increases the sensitivity of that production system.**
When there are less kanban in motion, there is less of a buffer between processes and therefore the system is more sensitive to disruption.

fig. 19

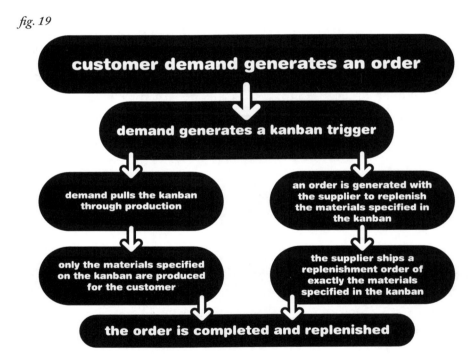

When the term kanban or kanban card is used, it is describing a specific tag affixed to goods or materials. Despite the prevalence of advanced software systems, it is still common practice for contemporary Lean manufacturers to employ kanban cards. In conjunction with electronic signals that originate the pull of materials (kanban triggers), a kanban card will travel with the order through production while an order is dispatched to the supplier for replenishment.

For manufacturers who have made the jump to completely electronic kanban systems, the pitfalls associated with physical cards such as lost or incorrectly entered cards are a thing of the past. All kanban triggers and subsequent movement through production can be tracked easily and with a high degree of accuracy. This information can then be integrated into an enterprise resource planning (ERP) software suite, and the visibility—and therefore responsiveness of the entire system—can be improved even more. Of course, implementation incurs cost, though new ERP software packages can be tailored to fit the *e-kanban* model and the organization, meaning that cost can be justified by gains in visibility, communication, and flexibility.

Heijunka Box

The *heijunka box* is a visual scheduling tool used in conjunction with the kanban system of material replenishment. It's a practical expression of the smoothing of production (heijunka), and an essential coordination tool.

Most commonly employed as a wall schedule, the heijunka box is a grid-style layout of cubbies or pigeonholes. Kanban cards are placed in the holes to visually organize their flow through the production process.

Columns and rows represent periods of time and processes. Each of the kanban cards moves with products through the production process (remember, under the kanban system, no goods are to be moved without a kanban card). Cards are stored in the heijunka box for retrieval. At a glance, supervisors and production staff can see exactly where product batches are in the production process, what remains to be done, and what the status is of each product at any given point in time.

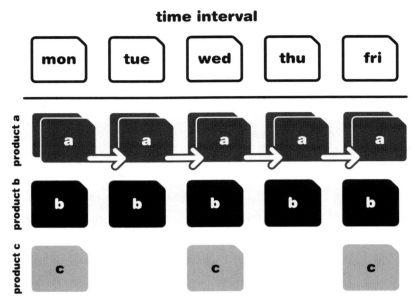

fig. 20 : A model of a heijunka box. Each of the cards represents a product traveling through production. The repeating patterns demonstrate at a glance that production is even and flowing. This time interval is set to days of the week, but a box could be as micro as thirty-minute intervals if need be.

Takt Time

Takt time is yet another tool in the Lean practitioner's toolkit. 'Takt' is best translated as "measure time," and it is a measurement of unit production time relevant to the rate of customer demand. Takt time is *not* a recording or calculation of the actual duration of unit production, rather a metric that identifies production flow and prescribes production line parameters. Best described as the work time between two units, takt calculations are not solely relevant to the world of manufacturing and production.

Control functions such as testing, quality control, and sampling can be described and measured with takt calculations. Administrative functions too, such as call service operations or inquiry response operations, can benefit from takt calculations. In this way, takt time is an evaluation tool used to examine processes while staying distinct from other tools.

Takt time is calculated based on the following formula:

fig. 21

Where :

T = Takt time

Ta = Work time per period (net available work expressed as time)

D = Customer demand or simply demand (expressed as production units)

Consider the following example:

A manufacturing firm has a shift length of eight hours (480 minutes). From this 480-minute gross, lunch allotments and breaks are deducted along with other business related nonproduction time.

fig. 22

Gross Time	480
Lunch	-30
Breaks	-30
Meetings	-10
Inspections	-10
	400

The result, 400 minutes, is the ***net available time to work.*** If customer demand was at 200 units per day (assuming one shift in a day), then the takt time becomes T = 400/200 (T = Ta/D) or a takt time of 2 minutes per part.

Once a takt time calculation is in place, it can be applied to a host of business tasks, and this confers a number of visibility and waste reduction benefits. When measured with a takt calculation, production at all levels can be matched to the calculated standard. This means that any workstations or production stages that are underperforming are easily identified. Underperformance can stem from a variety of sources, but no matter the cause, it is bottlenecking production. These bottlenecks are generating waste events, and once they become visible, corrective action can be taken.

Additionally, takt calculations focus solely on value-added activities. When calculating takt time for a given process, there is little room for non-value-added activities such as line changing, machine setup, and retooling. This value-added mindset encourages decision-making that best benefits the business and the customer and reduces waste.

In the same vein, the takt system leaves no room for the removal of incomplete goods from the production line. This is a value-added focus first, but in a secondary capacity it also translates into fewer opportunities for transport and motion waste events, as well as shrinkage due to inadvertent damage or loss.

As a standardization measure, takt calculations ensure that production level workers are repeating the same actions on a daily basis. This specialization breeds mastery and efficiency. When front line employees have to spend less time adapting to new processes on a frequent basis, total productivity increases.

All of these benefits come with a word of caution, however: detailed time calculations produce inflexible thinking and if not executed correctly can cause unanticipated issues. For example, if customer demand soars, an adjustment to the takt calculations means that some tasks will simply take too long in their current configuration.

One way to remedy the situation would be to split the same process over multiple workstations. This is a double-edged sword in the sense that additional workstations mean retooling and line-changing downtime, as well as time consumed by production line workers adapting to the change in processes. There is no prescribed right answer in this case; solutions should be developed on a case-by-case basis and should be tailored to fit the business and the industry.

Takt planning also places a high level of reliance on the integrity of machines and workstations. As a result, when one station breaks down, it can cause disruption throughout the entire production line, and this downtime coupled with recovery measures can be a costly prospect. This can be mitigated by factoring in buffer time for each unit; however, buffer time can be difficult to justify, because it's non-value-added (a firm can't charge their customers more because they have to insulate their production lines from unforeseen interruptions). The result is that decision makers and planners must strike a balance between factoring in reasonable buffer times and maintaining a focus on waste reduction and productivity.

Another consideration for takt implementation is the increased number of cycles that are generated when takt time is shortened. Following the takt formula, as demand (D) increases without net time available to work (Ta) also increasing, then the final takt value (T) will be lower. Lower takt time means more cycles and higher stress on systems, machines, and personnel.

Finally, takt time calculations are most effective when used with production lines that have benefited from production leveling. Production leveling is covered in more depth later on in this chapter, but to summarize the downside here, production leveled processes can suffer from increased amounts of inflexibility.

fig. 23

Takt Time

STRENGTHS	WEAKNESSES
• Inefficiency, waste, and bottlenecks are made visible	• Poor responsiveness to unanticipated high demand increases
• Focuses on value-added activities	• Workstation or machine failure can result in expensive line downtime
• Reduces shrink, damage, and loss	• Short takt times can result in high stress on parts and people
• Increases productivity through standardization	• Introduces inflexibility through production leveling

Just-in-Time

Just-in-Time (JIT) is a production strategy designed to reduce costs through reducing in-process inventory or **raw materials** inventory for production firms, which also reduces overall carrying costs. This concept can be extended to include the on-hand inventory for retail firms or any organization that holds inventory.

Just-in-Time is a waste reduction method and is a critical part of a culture of continuous improvement (read "Lean"). The overriding theory behind JIT is simple: the carrying costs associated with the storage of unused inventory are a wasteful use of resources. The JIT philosophy itself is a combination of statistics, behavioral science, management, industrial engineering, and production management. These disciplines have come together to redefine how inventory relates to management and how it is defined on the business level.

JIT uses the carrying costs associated with inventory to expose issues with manufacturing or excess production. The idea is that removing inventory exposes preexisting manufacturing issues, and a focus on reducing on-hand inventory will not only expose these issues but also preempt them in the effort to constantly improve these protocols and procedures. This means that firms are pushed to not only *require* fewer inventories but to *generate* fewer inventories.

The overall focus of JIT is to have "the right material at the right time at the right place in the exact right amount to fulfill business needs" without the inventory safety net or the creation of wasteful **safety stock**. For firms heavily entrenched in more traditional methods, a more incremental change is necessary to achieve the true cost savings associated with JIT methods. JIT requires sophisticated levels of cooperation and communication between suppliers and buyers to coordinate delivery and production and, as such, is not a cost-effective solution for some organizations. In many cases relationships between members of a supply chain network need to be improved before Just-in-Time production and inventory can be implemented.

Small Lot Production

Small lot production is the production implementation of flexibility. It shortens lead times, meaning manufacturing facilities can not only respond more quickly to changing demand but also produce a wider array of products. This also helps reduce wastes associated with excess inventory, motion, transportation, and overprocessing. Small lot production is also a critical component of Just-in-Time inventory. Conceptually as well as in practice, there is the overriding focus on waste elimination and the reduction of cost through the reduction of inventory and associated carrying costs.

Small lot production is a core component of the pull production system. Coupled with the line changeover shortening practices covered in the next segment, it becomes clear how Lean production overcomes the traditional barriers associated with push production. Large batches and long line changes were so inhibitive to production that the entire process was shaped around conforming to and reducing the impact of such obstacles.

All of the tools explained thus far, and the remaining portions of this chapter, together in unison rewrite the rules of production and present a highly capable and responsive alternative. Small lot production means not only that wasteful overproduction and safety stock is eliminated, but also that fluctuations in demand can be addressed more readily.

Push production practices are slow to respond to unanticipated changes in demand, while pull production, employing small lot production practices, simply ceases production of the unneeded goods and changes over to the production of those in demand.

There is, however, an unavoidable negative consequence in the area of setup time. This could be represented as line changing, cutting head replacement, workstation staging, etc. Companies that have decided to switch to small lot production need to analyze their setup times in regard to best practices, facility layouts, and production scheduling to determine the best course of action in minimizing downtime due to production setup changes. Setup time varies wildly due to the type of production, materials, type of process, and processing level, so there is no one formula for determining setup time optimization. The implementation of *single minute exchange of die* (SMED) measures (next section) addresses the inevitable increases of setup time and line changeovers.

Single Minute Exchange of Die

With the reduction in batch sizes and increase in flexibility that the pull production method provides, new issues are brought to the forefront. During mass production that utilizes large batches, the *economies of scale* are leveraged to spread the cost of inevitable line changeovers out over as many units as possible, and line changes are scheduled to be as minimally disruptive as possible. When the size of the batch production shrinks, the number of line changes that are necessary increases substantially, and in the kaizen spirit of reducing both downtime and D.O.W.N.T.I.M.E. waste, methods of efficient changeover follow the decision to switch to small batch production.

"Single minute" does not literally mean that all line changes should have a duration of only one minute; rather it means that they should not exceed ten minutes (single digit minute duration). While there is no prescribed solution that fits all industries, products, and production lines, the SMED concept encourages the critical examination of line change procedures and focuses waste elimination efforts on the processes that surround production and not just the production line itself.

The history of the SMED program also serves as the concept's most instructive model. During the 1960s, Toyota was finding that the most difficult line changes to perform were those of the die used in their largest car body transfer machines. These massive stamping machines utilized die that weighed multiple tons and had to be installed with millimeter scale tolerances. First attempts were not promising. The die had to cool before it could be removed, then it was transferred via overhead crane out of the stamping machine. The replacement die was then lowered back down—also via crane—and set first using operator eyesight and then a series of measurements around the entire assembly. The process could take days to complete, and throughout this time the line was completely down.

To improve the process, a number of innovations were applied. First, precision measuring devices were installed on the transfer assembly itself. This meant that the operators no longer had to use their eyesight to set multiple tons of steel into millimeter scale tolerances. Though a relatively minor change, this modification to the die-swapping process reduced the overall time to less than two hours. Further observation yielded further innovation, and the process was reduced to less than ten minutes. Scheduling and staging the crane and replacement die for efficient swap, as well as other changes, resulted in the drastic time savings.

In addition to the obvious reduction in changeover time, a host of other benefits are associated with proper implementation of SMED.

- Even if the number of changeovers increases, machine work rates still increase due to the reduction in setup times (net gain).
- Standardized and accurate setup eliminates defective production due to setup error.
- The defect rate is also decreased due to the decreased need for trial runs and calibrating runs.
- Quality is improved due to fully regulated operating conditions in advance (machines "hit the ground running" and require less tweaking)

- Simpler setups improve safe working conditions and necessitate fewer tools/labor costs.

The key benefit, however, remains the ability to respond to changes in production needs quickly and flexibly without incurring prohibitive amounts of cost and thus losing competitive edge.

While the specifics of successful SMED implementation vary from production line to production line, the key is to differentiate internal setup operations from external ones. *Internal setup operations* are those that require the complete shutdown of machines. Internal setup operations stop production by halting the line. *External setup operations* are those that can and should be completed, and should be, completed while the machine is running. External setup operations can be performed without any impact on production; the machine keeps running and the line keeps moving.

When implementing SMED methods across the production processes, decision makers should attempt to convert as many internal setup operations as possible into external ones instead. While this may not necessarily reduce the actual setup time in terms of minutes, it does reduce the impact of changeovers on the production line through the ability to make changes "on the fly."

Total Quality Management

Total quality management (TQM) is a company top-to-bottom practice that is designed to improve quality at every level. TQM came about as a parallel to the Lean method, and while it is a distinct program, it fits the Lean model. As we know, Lean strives for continuous improvement and for producing the highest quality product at the best cost while eliminating waste, and these are also core concepts of TQM. The customer's needs are the final determining factors in quality, and therefore the customer's "voice" is coupled with the demand that pulls goods through the production process. Voice of the Customer (VOC) then defines quality as meeting or exceeding customer expectations in all areas. This includes not only production of goods matching the customer's specifications, but on-time delivery, service, and value.

It is clear that the TQM program is incompatible with the traditional "push" production systems that produced products based on anticipated demand with inventory techniques such as safety stock and excess inventory designed to cover delivery shortfalls. In understanding VOC as a component of TQM programs, we see many of the components of Lean-like practices working in unison.

TQM is a generalized quality control system that many readers may already be familiar with. It prescribes the practical aspects of the tools and methods that Lean also encourages. For a number of American organizations, TQM was a first brush with the concepts of customer-centric planning and supply chain coordination. An overview of TQM could, in many cases, stand in for an overview of Lean, and demonstrates how similar the two quality improvement programs are.

When utilizing the TQM method, all stages of the supply chain must interact with one another in the broad view capacity. Two departments cannot have conflicting goals, as this lack of focus on the overall goal can create waste in the form of non-value-added activities and a decrease in quality for the customer. Miscommunication between elements of the supply chain can also distort perception of the customer's needs so radically that the goods produced no longer match the customer's needs.

The supply chain and manufacturing departments must be flexible, because the needs of the customer can change. The entire process must be visible to management as well as to employees at all levels to prevent misinformation, allow for the identification of waste, and prevent instances of the ***bullwhip effect*** or the magnification of non-value-added activities, errors, and misinformation throughout the supply chain. And of course, a culture of continuous improvement means that the drive for consistent and always higher quality means that the voice of the customer will always be the focus.

The High Cost of Poor Quality

"The bitterness of poor quality lingers long after the sweetness of low price has faded."

— Brian Thomas, *management professional*

The cost of poor quality is a serious concern for any organization striving to maintain a competitive edge. It can also be a concern for companies attempting to cut costs; the lowest-cost option should never compromise quality. An understanding of the costs associated with poor quality is most immediately pertinent to the manufacturing industry, but the cost of poor quality is a concept that permeates all fields. Quality-related issues can be divided into four general categories that identify the costs associated with low quality (Figure 24).

Incurring some costs to suppress others is not a novel concept, and in these cases it is almost an essential one. The level of quality monitoring and prevention of defects is dependent on many factors: the complexity of manufacturing or assembly, the needs of the customer, difficulty in sampling or assessing raw materials, work in progress, or finished goods. If the costs of reworking a part, retooling, rescheduling production, or scrap are costing twenty percent, forty percent, or in some complex reworking scenarios one hundred and fifty percent of the product's original cost of production, then instituting monitoring and prevention plans is essential.

While costs to mitigate defects are not directly value-added (the customer will spend the same on a part from a lot that was sampled as one that was not) the lack of serious quality control measures can be considerably harmful to a company's operations. If customers cannot receive a part or a product manufactured to the specifications they requested, then their business will follow them elsewhere. Likewise, if a company cannot determine what the source of defects is within the production line or cannot track success in improvements to defect reduction, then there can be no certainty of the quality of finished goods.

fig. 24

Quality Associated-Costs

1. External Failure Cost

- Defects found by the customer
- Returns, complaints, loss of perception of quality

2. Internal Failure Cost

- Defects found "in house," before delivery to the customer
- Scrapping, reworking, retooling, downtime

3. Monitoring Cost

- The cost of determining quality standards compliance
- Measuring , evaluating, sampling, reviewing

4. Prevention Cost

- This is the cost of preventing poor quality
- Inspections, quality control teams, planning, etc.

Facility Layout & Uniform Plant Loading

In respect to facility layout for production there are many considerations to take into account. It is also important to remember that facility layout is not set in stone; it is a concept that must be revisited periodically in the spirit of continuous improvement. Each element of the production process has an impact on the others, so changing the characteristics or position of a single workstation can impact the entire production line. There are four types of facility layouts detailed in the following graphic.

Fixed Position Layout

Fixed position facility layouts are an appropriate choice for the manufacture of products that cannot be moved during the production process. This could be due to size or to the installation nature of the product. Some examples of static products are civil engineering projects, oceangoing vessels, airplanes, spacecraft, oil rigs or derricks, and some mining equipment. Here the challenges associated with the supply chain are twofold. Not only do the assembly components and raw materials have to be at the appropriate site at the appropriate time, but they must arrive in the appropriate order.

Fixed Position Layout

fig. 25 : Fixed product layouts are most applicable to the production of goods that cannot be feasibly moved through a production line (such as aircraft or large structures). This facility layout focuses instead on moving workstations as needed around a static product until production is complete.

In this layout, workstations are often organized around the product during the production process. Unlike traditional production in which the product moves through the process physically as well as in the sense of process completion in a fixed layout facility plan, it is instead the workstations that physically move around the product while it is "moving" through the production process. This also presents challenges in the form of logistics, setup time, and supply chain responsiveness. Because of the size and often the complexity of products manufactured using this layout, the volume produced is usually very low, and there is a high level of customization available to the customer due to the "made to order" nature of the processes.

Product Layout

Product facility layout is more in line with what is normally considered traditional production. This is akin to the assembly line model in which many similar or nearly identical products are produced rapidly. The production of automobiles, electronics, grocery items, and countless consumer and commercial goods are produced using a product layout facility plan.

This layout excels at producing one or two products at high volume with very little differentiation. This configuration also simplifies quality control, planning, scheduling, and supervision. It is the most easily automated method of manufacture due to its highly repetitive nature.

Although speed and cost are strong attributes, this facility layout suffers from a low level of responsiveness and varying lead times. Setup times can be long, and reactions to changing customer needs can be sluggish. Additionally, each workstation relies on the one before it, so waste in the process can be easily amplified if a defective part is pulled (pull production system) through each workstation causing wasteful transportation and motion throughout, ultimately producing a product that requires scrap or rework. In this same vein, stoppages or bottlenecks at one workstation directly affect the productivity of workstations further down the line. The worst-case scenario of this domino-style effect would be complete line stoppage or entire batch production of defective products.

fig. 26

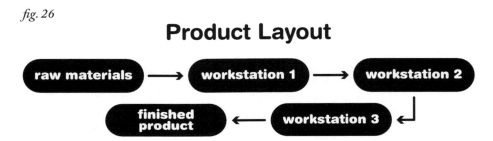

Product Layout

Process Layout

Process facility layouts are the best choice for low volumes of products that have high levels of differentiation. In this type of production, different products have such varying needs that the creation of a line process or sequential production process would be difficult and costly. In a facility layout that utilizes the process design, workstations and resources are grouped by production process. In this way individual products may begin the process at different workstations and follow different paths, depending on the specifications for their completion. This results in the ability to produce a wide range of various products. This configuration is evident in service industries as well. Consider a department store or grocery store. Products are stored on shelves, and different customers will move to different departments (read "process workstations") depending on their needs. Different customers will travel different paths, and the department store will be able to provide a large assortment of varying products. Customers can travel from area to area at will; each department is set up to be ready for their shopping needs.

There are, however, numerous challenges and disadvantages associated with this method of facility layout. Because of the diverse nature of the different workstation groups, work in progress, inventory, and processing times will be higher on average than dedicated production lines. Products will spend more time waiting or in transit from one department or workstation group to the next. This also means that material handling costs will be higher and products will need to be in transit from one workstation group to the next more often. Scheduling and planning, too, becomes more complicated considering that multiple types of products may be queued to a single workstation or workstation group. This can mean significant and varying downtime during setup changes and line adjustments. In the visual example below, each workstation group represents a process or department for the production of a different product.

Process Layout

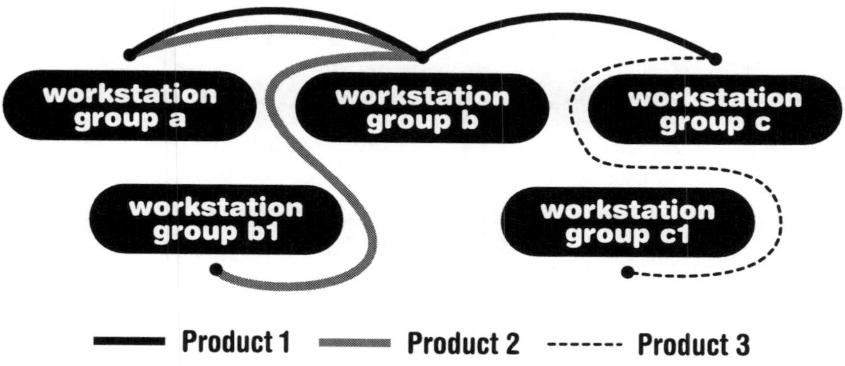

fig. 27: Each product enters the production cycle based on which workstations are required to produce finished goods. Not all workstations will be needed for each product.

Cellular Layout

Cellular facility layouts strive to maximize both flexibility and efficiency by pairing the product layout concept with that of the process layout. In this layout, products are grouped into categories based on processing characteristics. These categories, or product families, determine the arrangement of small product layout groups, or groups of product-oriented workstations, called cells. The cells then utilize the product layout that is tailored to the production needs of that cell's assigned product family. In this way the diversity afforded by the process layout can still be tapped in the form of the individual cells.

fig. 28

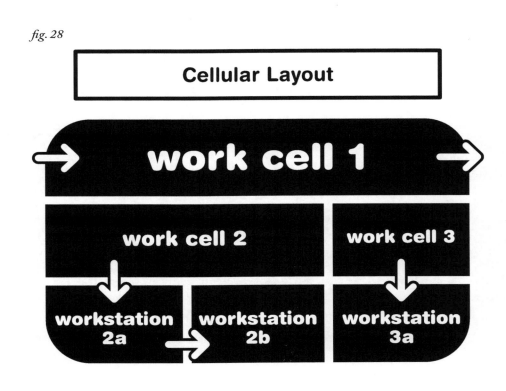

fig. 29

Summary of Production Layouts

1. Fixed Position Layout

- Used for production of static products
- Airplanes, homes, installations

2. Product Layout

- Used for production of static products
- Airplanes, homes, installations

3. Process Layout

- Used for production of low-volume products with high differentation
- Service industries, retail, studios

4. Cellular Layout

- Combines product and process layouts for efficiency
- Groups products into families for efficiency

Production Leveling

Production leveling is a method of reducing the waste generation of unevenness in production flow. As the name implies, production leveling activities are designed to allow the production of goods at a predictable and constant rate. The task of production leveling is a simple one during periods of constant demand, but in reality customer demand often fluctuates.

Production and demand are two sides of the same coin. When implementing production leveling methods, decision makers can either target the production side of the coin or the demand side. When leveling production from the production side, the approach can be further refined to "leveling by volume" or "leveling by product mix."

Leveling by Volume

Production leveling by volume operates on the key assumption that if volumes of production are altered to meet fluctuating demand, then unevenness is incorporated into the system, and therefore waste is generated during periods of "forced" capacity production. Instead of tailoring production to short-term shipments, manufacturers maintain their expected production output, overproducing when orders don't output (causing them to carry inventory) and underproducing when short-term orders exceed output.

These latter periods of underproduction would be offset—in theory—by the carried inventory that was generated by the production that exceeded short-term demand. This intentional production of surplus (and associated costs) is counterintuitive to many aspects of the Lean model.

Taking a broad view, however, the carried inventory simplifies the production process, and simplicity *is* a core component of Lean. It creates an evenness to production so that the rate of production isn't fluctuating, and even though carrying inventory does incur costs, it is the role of decision makers within the organization to determine which activity costs more: fluctuating production capacity or carrying inventory.

Additionally, while leveling by volume *does* ignore short-term demand, the organization is fulfilling the average demand in the long run by rolling in carried inventory to cover shortages when demand is high, and carrying that same inventory as a form of safety stock when demand is low.

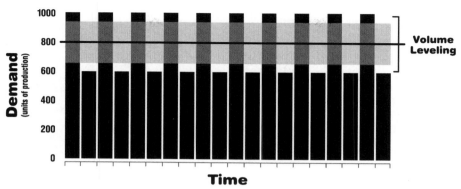

fig. 30: Cyclic demand shown over time. The shaded area represents the fulfillment of overall demand, through excess production and insufficient production throughout that period. The black line at the 800-unit level indicates the leveled average volume of production.

Leveling by Product Mix

Though in practice production leveling by product mix is a different approach than leveling by volume, the two methods may be used together as costs dictate. Leveling by product mix is largely unique to organizations that employ the pull production system and that benefit from short line changeovers such as those gained from a SMED program. The flexible nature of small batch production, coupled with the ability to change lines frequently for a low cost, compounds flexibility further still.

Due to the high degree of flexibility, a wider variety of fluctuating demand for various goods can be fed into production without the significant increase in costs associated with more traditional production lines. To handle the complicated scheduling, a kanban production system guided by a detailed heijunka box maintains evenness of flow throughout the entire production line and efficiently coordinates complex production schedules.

Implementation Techniques

To ensure that production leveling efforts are productive and impactful, there is a prescribed method of bringing production to the summit of responsiveness and value. A gradual reduction in batch size and increase in the ability to meet short-term changes in customer demand are slowly factored into the production system and the results build on one another.

The following tiers of production organization are incrementally introduced into the production cycle.

- **Fixed Sequence/Fixed Volume (Green Stream/Red Stream)**
  Products in the mix with predictable or constant demand are added to production accordingly with fixed sequence production (green). Red stream (fixed volume) products are those with demand that regularly fluctuates. This differentiation ensures that the proper treatment is given to each aspect of the product mix. Once a green stream/red stream program is introduced, it benefits from the *economies of repetition*, and can be factored into normal production.

- **Fixed Sequence/Unfixed Volume**
  The stream sequences are maintained, but actual sales data, (short-term demand changes) are factored in to impact the production cycle.

- **Unfixed Sequence/Fixed Volume**
  This method employs small batch sizes (fixed volume), and a diverse product mix (unfixed sequence).

- **Unfixed Sequence/Unfixed Volume**

  Here we have an ideal state where the production line is so responsive and flexible that the batch size on all products is one. This is termed "single piece flow" and is the pinnacle of Lean manufacturing. Essentially on-demand manufacturing, customer demand is always met with 100 percent accuracy, production is always 100 percent even, and the production line is a Lean machine that generates nothing but value.

It is worth noting that the Toyota Production System never achieved single piece flow production.

Demand Leveling

On the other side of the coin is production and demand, and production leveling through the influence of demand deals with a radically different set of approaches and practices.

One approach is for the manufacturer to carefully control the sales pipeline all the way down to the customer. This "door to door" approach ensures an extremely high level of predictability with demand while building the long-term value of the customer. Sales staff are agents of the manufacturer or licensed dealers, and at every level of the sales mix the manufacturer has some measure of control.

During the development of the Toyota Production System, Toyota used this method to high-impact effect. Sales staff worked closely with customers and built lasting and valuable relationships. On the production side of things, customer orders (demand) were met almost on a vehicle-by-vehicle basis, and Toyota was in control of the production-to-sales-to-delivery process, meaning that not only was the Voice of the Customer loud and clear, but the rate of demand was highly predictable.

Another similar—though distinct—approach to production leveling through demand management involves a close relationship with the sellers or retailers, and a deep understanding of their systems and processes as well as their sales data and trends related to same. Thinking back to demand amplification planning, POS (point of sale) data can be a particularly helpful resource in this respect.

Other Tools : Six Sigma

Though not a facet of the Lean method, the *Six Sigma quality* improvement system is common within the sphere of the production industry and can be paired with Lean with impressive results.

The statistical basis for the Six Sigma quality improvement program is too exhaustive to delve into here; rather, a plain English overview is offered. In his book *Winning*, Jack Welch, giant conglomerate GE's former CEO, states that Six Sigma was "adopted from Motorola in 1995 and continues to [be] embraced today." He also goes on to laud its abilities to enhance an organization's operational efficiency, improving productivity and lowering costs.

The program, like Lean, is a top-to-bottom design of an organization's operations and structure that strives to improve customer satisfaction, lower costs, and create better leaders. It also focuses on product lines and production processes to reduce waste, variation, and distortion or errors within the supply chain. All of these characteristics are set to the goal of creating the highest level of customer satisfaction and, therefore, the most competitive edge.

Six Sigma adherent Jack Welch goes on to discuss Six Sigma's practical applications and results. Six Sigma excels at removing variation and defects from repetitive tasks. This is a basic but effective application and applies to many industries other than manufacturing and production. Service industries, too, can benefit from Six Sigma uniformity in reducing defects in areas such as billing, customer service, and supply chain response time. This more basic level of application has a positive side effect on the organization as well: it trains the ranks of management to become high-level critical thinkers and improves discipline.

Six Sigma is also a powerful tool for the planning and production of massively complex projects such as turbines and aerospace assemblies. It is used to identify inconsistencies and irregularities before large amounts of resources are committed to the project. This application is certainly more advanced and requires the expertise of scientists and engineers well-versed in the statistical language of Six Sigma. Expert Jack Welch cautions, though, that it is not a program that is designed to be applied to the creative process or to one-time transactions. Statistical inspection of the product design process, for example, would be far more of a hindrance than a help and would generate unnecessary cost.

Other Tools : Lean Six Sigma

As the elements that make up Lean and Six Sigma are explored, the pairing of the two becomes an obvious inevitability. Both methodologies elevate the focus on the customer to the level of guiding principle, and both focus on quality, waste reduction, and cost savings. Though the basics of *Lean Six Sigma* will be covered here, a full exploration of this dynamic pairing is beyond the scope of this text.

Both methodologies offer a diverse range of tools: Lean offers a flexible approach, a broad view, a culture of continuous improvement, and a vigilant mindset. Six Sigma offers a bevy of high-powered statistical tools and analyses, a core obsession with quality, a focus on staff hierarchy, and a critical thinking mindset second to none.

When deployed in tandem, the hybrid approach of Lean Six Sigma can truly elevate an organization to new heights of productivity, quality assurance, and customer satisfaction. Decision makers can pick and choose which tools are best for their organization, while adhering to standardization protocols that lay out which elements best augment each other. While sometimes doubling the size of a toolbox means finding the right tool for the job, Lean Six Sigma has been streamlined and developed in such a way that tools and processes dovetail into one another. With the wealth of information available, and the extensive history that both systems have, decision makers are able to easily ascertain what works and what doesn't in terms of tools and processes.

Although Lean Six Sigma is sometimes criticized for requiring massive amounts of administration, training, and planning, implementing it not only pays for itself many times over, but also makes a bold investment in processes, people, and quality that builds and preserves a lasting competitive edge. The gains to be had in the areas of process improvement, organizational thinking, and unprecedented quality control are more than worth the trade-off in time, effort, and disruption.

To Recap

- The pull production system is a core element of Lean manufacturing. In contrast to traditional push production, where demand is forecasted and "pushes" materials through the production cycle, pull production focuses on actual demand.

- To evaluate the current state of systems, and to benchmark current conditions for later comparisons of progress, the value stream mapping collection of tools can be deployed. Consisting of a variety of technical analysis tools, value stream mapping seeks to differentiate value-added and non-value-added aspects of processes within the value stream.

- To coordinate and control the replenishment and tracking of products through the production cycle, the use of a system of kanban cards ensures that once materials are used for production, an order is generated for their replenishment. When in place, a kanban system maintains level production as well as consistent replenishment and availability of materials for production. To schedule the complex kanban system, a heijunka box is deployed. This is a wall schedule broken into a grid pattern that organizes products in relation to time intervals of production.

- To determine a flow of production, the calculation of a takt time is used to determine a production rate. Just-in-Time methods can also be used to create an even flow. Just-in-Time is the scheduling of goods and materials to put the exact right amount in the right place at exactly the right time. JIT methods reduce waste by eliminating the costs of carrying unneeded inventory and unnecessary transport and waiting.

- All of these concepts support and enable the pull production system's reliance on small lot production. Small lot production is a flexible and responsive production system that focuses on smaller batches that meet demand and do not create waste in the form of excessive production or unneeded inventory.

- Additionally, Single Minute Exchange of Die (SMED) programs strive to reduce line downtimes due to changeovers. Together, all of these concepts contribute to effective and value-added small lot production.

- If value for the customer is a focus of operations, then so too should be quality of finished goods. Not only is quality an important aspect of value, poor quality is often costly and generates significant amounts of waste. Total Quality Management and a focus on the Voice of the Customer are both aspects that an organization should embody if customer value is at the forefront.

- Six Sigma is a quality control and systems improvement method that values statistical analysis and can be combined with the Lean framework to produce the hybrid program, Lean Six Sigma. Lean Six Sigma draws from both methodologies to produce a quality-focused management program that relentlessly attacks inefficiency and waste.

- No matter the field of manufacturing, facility layout contributes to overall process efficiency. Facility layout can be broken into four rough categories: fixed position, product, process, and cellular layouts. Each of these layouts has strengths and weaknesses based on the goods being produced. Once an effective facility layout is implemented, production leveling can be initiated. Attempting production leveling activities without first optimizing the efficiency of production will result in significant amounts of unnecessary additional work.

- Production leveling is the process of reducing variance in the production process, and two approaches exist: production leveling through production (volume and product mix) or production leveling through demand.

Key Questions (Answers on pg. 137)

1. The pull production system differs from traditional push production in what way?

   a) pull production requires much higher cycle speeds

   b) pull production requires less labor

   c) pull production paces production with demand

   d) there is no difference

2. Which of the following statements best describes value stream mapping?

   a) value stream mapping is a method of trickling value across the organization

   b) value stream mapping is a tool used to analyze the current state of processes and to identify waste

   c) value stream mapping is a tool used to calculate the production time per unit based on total available time

   d) value stream mapping is a management tool used to assist decision makers in efficient employee deployment

3. Kanban is a culture of continuous improvement.

   a) true

   b) false

4. When employing Just-in-Time inventory and supply chain protocols, which of the following statements is true?

a) goods and materials are scheduled in such a manner that only the amounts that are needed are moved throughout the supply chain, which *reduces* waste and carried inventory

b) goods and materials are scheduled in such a manner that only the amounts that are needed are moved throughout the supply chain, which *increases* waste and carried inventory

c) Just-in-Time drivers and warehouse workers are mandated to work twice as fast to keep up with tightened scheduling techniques

d) visual scheduling techniques enable a more level product flow using Just-in-Time methods

5. Which of the following is an advantage of small lot production?

a) smaller lot sizes increase the flexibility of production

b) smaller lot sizes reduce waste through the elimination of safety stock

c) smaller lot sizes are very responsive to changes in demand

d) all of the above

6. What is the purpose of executing a SMED (Single Minute Exchange of Die) program?

a) to increase the capacity of all transfer and stamping machines

b) to reduce the duration of downtime due to line changeovers

c) to reduce materials inventory throughout the supply chain

d) to level production by focusing on the demand component

7. Six Sigma is a Lean planning tool that is used to measure visibility.

a) true

b) false

8. The construction of a high-capacity passenger aircraft would probably be best carried out under which of the following facility layouts?

a) product layout

b) cellular layout

c) fixed position layout

d) process layout

| 3 |

The Lean Toolkit

In This Chapter

- Cause-and-effect tool Ishikawa diagram and physical pathway mapping in the form of a spaghetti plot are illustrated
- Poka-yoke mistake-proofing methods are covered in detail
- The decision to outsource and the Outsource Decision Matrix are presented
- The Theory of Constraints is discussed

Designed to augment the production processes laid out in the Lean manufacturing model detailed in the previous chapter, the following series of diagnostic and problem-solving tools are useful for improving business and production operations. Each of these tools has wide applications outside of the world of manufacturing and can be adapted to fit nearly any business in nearly any industry—even the service industry.

Ishikawa Diagrams (Fishbone Diagrams)

The versatile cause-and-effect diagrams developed by Kaoru Ishikawa are commonly known as fishbone diagrams or herringbone diagrams because of their distinctive repeating chevron shape. *Ishikawa diagrams* are generally suited to the process of identifying factors contributing to an overall effect, and that effect can be as large as the macro scale or as small as the micro.

Kaoru Ishikawa first developed the fishbone diagram in the 1960s as part of a trailblazing quality control program while he was with the now-famous manufacturer Kawasaki. Though fishbone diagrams were not a product of the Toyota Production System per se, they were rapidly adopted, and are now a commonplace tool in the Lean practitioner's toolkit.

More distinct applications find the Ishikawa diagram in use through the process of product design diagramming and quality defect prevention. As you will see, the construction and implementation of an effective fishbone diagram can be a time-consuming process. Multiple rounds of brainstorming and investigation should be planned and deployed carefully. When the root causes of a problem are fairly clear—machine inefficiency due to poor maintenance protocols, for example—a fishbone diagram is completely unnecessary and would cause more harm than good.

Fishbone diagrams are best used to disrupt a team's thinking and add a structured approach to a complex problem-solving process. When it seems like personnel are spinning their wheels tackling a complex effect on operations, that's the ideal time for application of a fishbone diagram.

Foundationally, the Ishikawa diagram groups together contributing factors or causes into categories that take a variety of production aspects into consideration. Known as the *5Ms* of manufacturing, the primary causal categories are as follows:

Machine

The *machine* category encompasses any equipment related to the process or needed to accomplish the job. This includes computer systems, production tools, methods of conveyance, etc.

Method

Methods are defined as the specific protocols that govern a process or operation. This could be as tangible as production specs, or as intangible as departmental policy. Even organizational policy could have a trickledown effect on day-to-day operations, so the methodology category can be complex to evaluate.

Material

Materials include all of the material aspects associated with a process. Raw materials, work in progress, and finished goods are obvious for the manufacturing sector, but less obvious are finishing materials, fasteners, and other ancillary components. Supplies and inventories should also be considered under the heading of materials.

Manpower

Manpower encompasses every person involved in the process, from the sets of hands on the production line to foremen, supervisors, management, and beyond if applicable. Contractors—though not employees—may still have a hand in the factors that bring about a certain effect, so they should not be left out of the equation. Likewise, critical staff from suppliers and customers can have an effect on an organization's operations. While recourse or corrective action may be limited in these cases, understanding the source of an impact means that decision makers aren't entirely powerless.

Measurement

Measurement describes the total of the data that is generated from or about the process. This not only includes normal, day-to-day business metrics, but monitoring and inspection-generated data as well. Data is only as accurate as the means by which it was gathered. A critical look at the tools and systems by which the data that is used in critical decision-making is an essential part of understanding the underlying causes of discrete effects.

It is worth mentioning that there is another widely recognized broad category that may be factored into causal classification: environment. Environment constitutes aspects such as temperature, geographic location, cultural norms, and all other miscellaneous aspects of production. Some interpretations of the 5Ms include as many as eight general cause categories, though the prevailing theory is that sticking to the basics is a safer and simpler approach.

As with all aspects of Lean, especially expressions of Lean outside the manufacturing and production sectors, *the business should never be stretched to fit the Lean model.* The Lean framework provides a guide and a best practices protocol system that gives decision makers the tools they need to build highly efficient businesses. The proposed causes of an effect are determined through a series of brainstorming sessions and through rigorous investigation. If a cause is determined that is unique to an industry or to an organization that defies classification as one of the 5Ms of manufacturing, that *does not* mean that it is invalid.

fig. 31

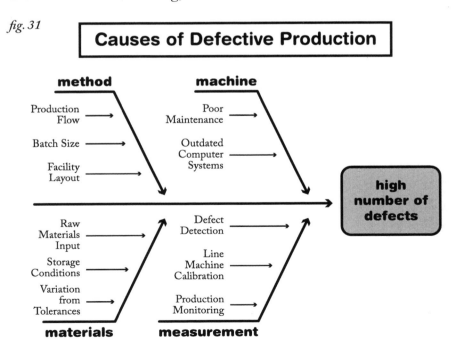

Adaptability and flexibility are core components of the Lean philosophy; industry leaders that truly understand these concepts should never shy away from repurposing the Lean toolkit to fit the needs of their business. In this respect, the 5W1H method can be particularly helpful in determining the root cause of a problem and shaping a fishbone diagram to fit the needs of the business. If a sixth category, environment, is appropriate for a particular industry or organization, then those fishbone diagrams should include an environment category. The same is true if there is a real need for seven or eight categories.

Tools Outside of Manufacturing : Fishbone Diagrams

Lean can be utilized across a wide spectrum of industries and business applications, many of which would have little use for the 5Ms of manufacturing. As a result, some other fields have adopted a more contextually appropriate set of causal criteria for their own fishbone diagrams.

The 8 P's of Marketing

- Product/Service
- Price
- Place
- Promotion
- People
- Process
- Physical Evidence
- Publicity

Sometimes condensed into a smaller list of core elements known as the 4 P's of Marketing (product, price, place, promotion), conventional fishbone diagram wisdom tells us that expanding the scope to include other, often overlooked aspects of the marketing mix can help decision makers determine the true root causes of issues.

The 4 S's of Service (not to be confused with the 5S Method found later in this text)

- Surroundings
- Suppliers
- Systems
- Skills

As evidenced by their application across a broad variety of industries, fishbone diagrams are highly effective tools for the structured investigation of cause and effect.

Spaghetti Plot

Spaghetti plots are versatile visual representations of data in the context of flow through a system. They are a clear companion to the Lean method with its focus on flow and evenness of production. The name comes from the long and wavy data depictions; the trends resemble long noodles laid out. When applied in a business environment, these visual charts are often known as workflow diagrams.

With statistical applications across all fields of science, from biology and zoology to meteorology and climatology, even the fields of medicine and pharmacology implement spaghetti plots to track flows. When the concept is applied to business, it can become a valuable tool that demonstrates exactly where waste events occur, not only in flow, but in inefficient transport, travel, and facility layout. In a more abstract sense, the flows of information and financials can also be fit to a spaghetti plot, and trend information as well as efficiency can be measured.

As with so many of the tools in the Lean toolkit, the goal of implementing spaghetti plots is to identify waste through the clear differentiation of value-added and non-value-added activity. When used to track a product through each production workstation, or for the layout of an office, workshop, or storage area, the overlaying lines can be instructive to decision makers in regard to where streamlining should occur and how to address layouts to consolidate efforts.

To build a spaghetti plot of a workspace, follow these steps:

1. Map the workspace as it physically occurs.
2. Merge the steps of a process with the map by plotting each step in the appropriate location on the map.
3. Connect the plotted points with arrows to indicate direction of flow.

The resulting chart is a visual display of the flow of work through the mapped space and can serve to inform layout and workflow decisions. Look for areas where lines cross one another frequently. These areas should be addressed and redesigned for a cleaner flow and to eliminate the additional labor of backtracking. If there is a single station that sees paths coming back multiple times, the work that is completed there should be investigated to see if it can be done at the same time to save wasted labor and movement.

fig. 32

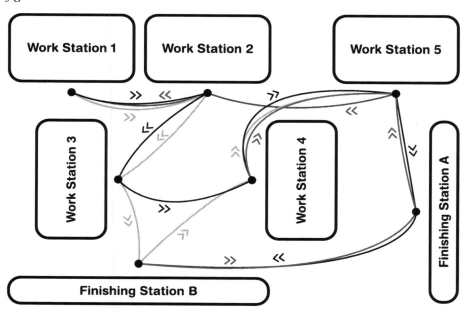

Poka-Yoke

While many of the Lean manufacturing tools focus on mechanical systems and methods of production, the concept of *poka-yoke* is a tool to correct the behavior of the human element within the production process. Deriving from the Japanese term yokuru poka (loosely meaning "avoid mistakes"), a poka-yoke is a process, protocol, or design that draws attention to—and reduces—the rate of human error. As a broader concept, a poka-yoke measure may not be a tangible design; it could be a behavioral conditioning or training protocol that has the same effect. In colloquial English, poka-yoke measures could be considered "foolproofing."

A poka-yoke measure is an intentional constraint, most often found in the form of a process step. The ring pull of a fire extinguisher is an example of a poka-yoke measure. In order to discharge a fire extinguisher, the ring pull must first be removed. This ensures that the canister cannot be accidentally discharged so that the fire suppressant inside is always ready in the event of a fire.

In the world of manufacturing and production, poka-yoke measures are implemented to reduce the rate of defective production right at the source. Successful poka-yoke design results in the immediate recognition and simple resolution of common human error. In practical applications, poka-yoke measures are tailored to the environment they are intended to impact.

Modifying production machinery to only accept production components in the correct orientation is a simple, yet effective, poka-yoke measure. Operators simply cannot load parts incorrectly; any attempt to do so is met with immediate feedback (the part doesn't fit).

Digital counters that track actions to ensure their conformity to specifications are more complicated poka-yoke measures. Preventing a welder from moving on to the next part unless a certain number of welds have been completed, for example, or modifying a workstation so that its tools can only be used in one way, are both poka-yoke measures.

The Decision to Outsource

Outsourcing is fast becoming a smart strategy for businesses in every industry. Outsourcing is the decision to work with a third party vendor, supplier, or service provider to carry out business activities. In many cases, this is simply a matter of contracting a firm that specializes in one business area to leverage the economies of *core competency*. This third party firm could be in the same neighborhood, across the country, or across the globe. Common activities that are outsourced include transportation, warehouse management, IT services, and customer service administration.

When an organization simply isn't competent in a business area, a serious examination of cost and value should arise in regard to the operations that make up the area of deficiency. Sometimes decision makers find that while the organization isn't equipped to handle these activities in their current state, or that the costs to reach a state where the organization's level of competency will make financial sense in the long run.

Other times, decision makers find that deficiencies in these areas are impossible to overcome in any manner that makes financial sense, and the decision to outsource or keep these activities in-house is put on the table.

Effective and successful outsourcing can provide a host of benefits. New talent and fresh minds are exposed to your organization, along with new ways of looking at operations and new efficiency methods. Once areas of deficiency or high cost are outsourced, the organization now has more resources to devote to areas of core competency and innovation.

Outsourcing can be a double-edged sword, however; poor outsourcing can lead to a loss of proprietary information, intellectual property, and the inclusion of components into the value chain that are below organizational quality standards. This makes the outsourcing decision a tricky one, and careful consideration should be taken throughout the process.

To aid in the determination of which operations or activities should be outsourced, the Outsourcing Decision Matrix is a valuable tool. This matrix is based on two critical pieces of information:

Criticality

How strategically important is this activity to maintaining the business' competitive edge and achieving strategic goals?

Impact

What is the impact of this activity on operations?

The combination of these two factors produces four possible overall categories for business activities:

- High Criticality, High Impact
- High Criticality, Low Impact
- Low Criticality, High Impact
- Low Criticality, Low Impact

High Criticality, Low Impact : Form a strategic alliance. These activities are vital to the success of the organization's long-term plans, but have little impact on the success of operations. This means that it is in the organization's best interest to retain the highest degree of control possible, while allowing another firm with a competitive advantage in their own field to handle the specifics. High criticality, low impact (HCLI) operations often include marketing and advertising, sales and promotion, and various distribution methods.

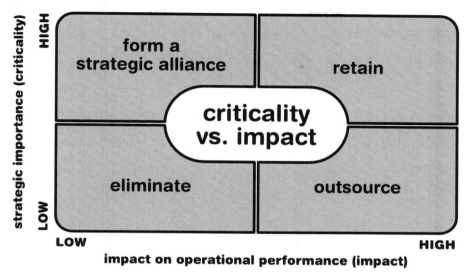

High Criticality, High Impact : These activities should be retained in-house. Due to the potentially catastrophic outcome of these activities being performed incorrectly, they should be kept in-house regardless of financial instability or cost deficiency. Operational and strategic health depend on on them, and therefore they are large contributors to competitive edge and in many cases constitute core competencies.

Low Criticality, High Impact : Activities that fall into this quadrant are prime candidates for outsourcing. These activities do not impact the strategic positioning of the company and therefore competitive edge, but they do have a high impact on the way in which operations are carried out. That means that transferring these activities to a third party vendor that specializes in them can free up time and resources for high criticality, high impact activities.

Activities such as distribution fall neatly into this category. Distribution of finished goods is a high impact activity; if goods don't reach downstream supply chain entities, then the organization has a problem, but as far as aspirations and core competencies are concerned, distribution has only a small role. It is something that must be done for the day-to-day operational success of the business, but it plays a limited role in the organization's strategic goals.

Low Criticality, Low Impact : Activities that have neither a major impact on operations nor a role in strategic planning should be examined closely. While you may not be able to eliminate these tasks completely, they should be scrutinized as potential sources of waste. Questions regarding LCLI activities should include the following:

- Why are these tasks undertaken?
- What, if anything, do they accomplish?
- What operations, activities, or processes would be affected if these LCLI activities were either eliminated or combined with higher criticality and higher impact activities?

The *Outsource Decision Matrix* is not a tool that is unique to Lean. It can be instructive for decision makers across a variety of industries who are assessing whether or not to outsource certain activities. For those adhering to Lean philosophy, the outsourcing decision is made more complex by some of the more rigorous Lean scheduling and production components. Based on the possible introduction of waste into the system, Lean organizations have an additional set of criteria by which to judge potential third party contractors.

It is important to remember that simply handing off cost and potential sources of waste to another company does not remove that cost and waste from the overall value stream. A reduction in value for the customer—whether as cost, quality, or some other value characteristic such as timeliness of delivery—will always occur if waste and inefficiency exist somewhere in the value stream and supply chain. The Lean principle of analyzing systems with a broad view aims to keep this aspect in the forefront of the minds of decision makers in all aspects of strategic decision-making.

The Theory of Constraints

The *Theory of Constraints* (TOC) is a management and production philosophy geared toward continuous improvement and goal-oriented achievement. While the TOC was developed in the Western world, contemporary Lean practitioners use it as a structured approach to continued improvement and production analysis. The Theory of Constraints is based on the premise that a system is *always* inhibited by at least one constraint. This premise is achieved through the following rationale: if there was nothing stopping the system from operating at full capacity (no constraints) then the system would generate value in increasing amounts *ad infinitum*. This is of course impossible; there is a physical ceiling to the performance of any system.

The Theory of Constraints seeks to find that physical ceiling through the focused and systematic elimination of artificial ceilings— constraints—that are impeding goal achievement. This is done through a series of structured focusing steps. As with all expressions of continuous improvement, the TOC focusing steps are designed to be applied cyclically. TOC employs its own form of Lean's kaizen, termed POOGI—process of ongoing improvement.

TOC Five Focusing Steps

1. Identify the system's constraint(s).
2. Decide how to exploit the system's constraint(s).
3. Subordinate everything else to the above decision(s).

4. Elevate the system's constraint(s).
5. If in the previous steps a constraint has been broken, go back to step 1).

The five focusing steps exist to narrow the approach to constraint reduction. In the modern business world, it can be easy to become overloaded with information, and the five focusing steps aim to cut straight to the issues. While the list of steps is simple enough, in practice quite a bit of planning and investigation can go into each step, especially if the process has been completed and the system has been elevated several times already.

A constraint is anything that is preventing consistent goal achievement. The TOC operates on the principle that there are not thousands of constraints within a system, but that the overreaching effects of constraints can be reduced to a handful. Constraints are broken down into two categories: internal and external. Internal constraints consist of subcategories such as equipment, people, and policy. An equipment constraint could be a mechanical threshold that is preventing higher levels of production. A constraint in regard to people could be a prevailing attitude or systemic lack of skill and understanding. Policy-based constraints come in the form of either written or unwritten protocols that limit the system's output.

External constraints are those that have an impact on the ability of the system to consistently achieve goals. These could be regulatory statutes, cultural norms, or public infrastructure shortcomings. While in some cases external constraints can be elevated and "broken," the TOC methodology focuses primarily on internal constraints as being the most productive to target.

When a constraint is elevated to the point that it is reduced completely, it is considered to be "broken." Once a constraint has been broken, the TOC's overriding premise is that there is always at least one other part of a system that is limiting or bottlenecking it. The five focusing steps should be applied to that system once again and the process starts over.

It is important to note that the broad constraint categories offer a multitude of sources of productivity and output loss, but in many instances these are *not* constraints in the TOC sense of the word. A constraint is a limiting factor that affects a system or a process. When a production line employee requires retraining, that is not a constraint. When the entire production line staff is insufficiently trained, that is a constraint. Likewise, a machine that suffers from frequent malfunction due to improper preventative maintenance is not a constraint. When the entire production line is made up of machines that are ill-suited to their tasks, that is a constraint.

Constraints can be seen as bottlenecks, and this is a key point to understand in regard to how the Theory of Constraints interacts with the Lean model. TOC focuses on the current system and what is limiting it. The goal of the five focusing steps is always to improve the system and raise the ceiling of production. This goal is in line with the Lean system, though TOC employs a different approach.

fig. 34

There is always at least one constraint limiting a system

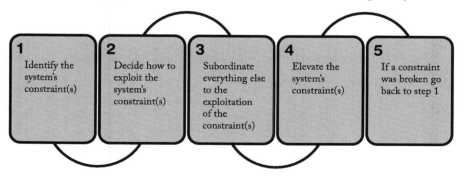

1	2	3	4	5
Identify the system's constraint(s)	Decide how to exploit the system's constraint(s)	Subordinate everything else to the exploitation of the constraint(s)	Elevate the system's constraint(s)	If a constraint was broken go back to step 1

Additionally, TOC differs from the Lean method in the sense that it is centered on processes and not products. The Lean manufacturing model and the pull production system are value-driven and, as a result, focus on products. Though distinct from the path of Lean philosophy, TOC still has practical applications in determining bottlenecks within a system and determining practical and sustainable ways to increase production capacity.

To Recap

- The Lean toolkit is a collection of techniques that can be applied to existing processes to gain insights or to spur innovation. All of the tools that accompany the Lean framework strive to uncover areas of waste, highlight potential increases in efficiency and productivity, and determine the root cause of problems plaguing the production process.

- The Ishikawa diagram, also known as the fishbone diagram, is a cause-and-effect mapping tool designed to investigate the causes of an effect at their most fundamental level.

- A spaghetti plot, or workflow map, visually details the paths taken by people or goods. Spaghetti plots are highly applicable across a wide variety of industries and can be used to map any activity that can be expressed as a flow.

- Poka-yoke measures, another Lean tool, are artificial constraints designed to turn activities into processes and to reduce the impact of human error on the production process.

- The Outsource Decision Matrix matrix is a quadrant matrix that helps decision makers determine which activities are candidates for outsourcing and which should be kept in-house. The tool also highlights those activities—low criticality, low impact activities—that should be addressed to determine potential sources of waste and inefficiency.

- The Theory of Constraints is a process improvement method that uses a series of focusing steps to identify and elevate constraints causing expensive bottlenecks within a system. Based on the premise that there is always at least one constraint that is limiting a system, the Theory of Constraints seeks to grow production capacity, efficiency, and productivity.

Key Questions (Answers on pg. 137)

1. Ishikawa diagrams, also known as fishbone diagrams, are used for what purpose?

   a) fishbone diagrams are a productivity mapping tool

   b) fishbone diagrams are a cost evaluation tool

   c) fishbone diagrams are a scheduling tool

   d) fishbone diagrams are a cause-and-effect tool

2. A spaghetti plot can be used to map which of the following?

   a) the path that materials take across the factory floor

   b) the path that employees take during production activities

   c) the path that employees take within an office setting

   d) all of the above

3. Poka-yoke measures are designed to reduce which of the following within the production process?

   a) costly employee overtime

   b) defects caused by human error

   c) machine deterioration due to poor maintenance

   d) waste events linked to transportation

4. The decision to outsource is complex and focuses on the relationship between impact and criticality.

   a) true

   b) false

5. The Theory of Constraints is a set of process improvement tools founded on which of the following?

a) the assumption that demand changes in a predictable manner

b) the assumption that production can be scaled to fit fluctuating demand

c) the premise that there is always at least one constraint that is limiting a system

d) the premise that a system starts out with no constraints, but that constraints are the product of human error

| 4 |

Implementation Considerations

In This Chapter

- The Lean focus on respect for people and the value of the workforce is discussed
- The 5S method for maintaining a Lean workplace is explained in detail
- The path to implementation and concerns for organizations attempting implementation are mapped out for organizations and decision makers

The implementation of Lean across a large organization is a massive task. In many cases it requires an entire restructuring of organizational culture. While many firms claim to value the input of employees on all levels; claim to vigilantly seek out and eliminate waste throughout operations; and claim to be agile, flexible, and visible, the reality is that the rigors of the Lean framework reflect a night-and-day change.

Just like the evaluation process for operations and processes, adoption and improvement is measured against results and high-level or macro targets. This is distinct from the framework of other adoption programs, which focus on the number of program adoption activities carried out. Even in implementation, the Lean program differentiates between value-added activities and wasteful ones.

This "hit the ground running" value differentiation mindset complicates the already complicated nature of Lean adoption within an organization. Implementation does not happen overnight. The extensive execution of pilot programs and training can be a costly process, and these steps represent a high barrier that must be overcome before the Lean culture can be spread across the organization.

Respect for People

A common thread that runs throughout the Lean business model is a firm commitment to respect for people. This is not a facility layout, value stream evaluation, or production method, and it is more than simply a culture of continuous improvement. It is apparent in business practices and decisions as well as interactions between management and employees on the production floor. Many companies claim that their greatest assets are their people, but a review of their policies and procedures would reveal that there is room for improvement.

There is an entire industry of literature devoted to management techniques and methods of improving efficiency and productivity among a workforce. The Lean business model does not strive to provide the answers to those questions, but a dedicated kaizen mindset ensures that everyone has a seat at the table. The developers of the Toyota Production System identified the fact that innovation springs from all levels of an organization and that respect for one's workforce garners respect for the workplace in return.

While it would stand to reason that an increased level of freedom, participation, and respect on the part of management toward employees would be a smooth transition for a workforce, somewhat surprisingly, individuals must be trained to contribute meaningfully. Innovation and continuous improvement are the twin engines of the Lean methodology; to achieve this, employee involvement at all levels and a competitive atmosphere of trialing and experimentation are essential.

In addition to management-employee relations barriers that may exist, a commitment to respecting people also means placing a high degree of trust in them. When management transfers trust to their employees, they lose a measure of control, but employees gain a high degree of autonomy within the organization. That is to say, employees are empowered to make appropriate decisions on their own. Operational and low-level strategic decisions are delegated, as are systems development efforts. To prime the organization for a desire to change and to adapt, a less risk-averse position must also be encouraged.

For some firms, all of these aspects can be terrifying prospects, but with a broad view mentality and an investment in their people, the development of staff as an organization's greatest asset is possible.

The 5S Method

Respect for people and respect for the workplace are goals that are as lofty as they are nebulous. In order to ensure that these two important aspects of Lean implementation are sufficiently met, the *5S method* is prescribed as a clear way to measure expectations for both employees and management.

Often hailed as the guidelines that enabled the timeliness of JIT manufacturing, the 5S method can come across as humble or underwhelming at first look, but is in fact a powerful workplace organization method. The 5S model derives its name from the five Japanese terms *seiri, seiton, seiso, seiketsu,* and *shitsuke*. Once written in Roman script, each of the words starts with the letter 'S,' hence the name. The 5 S's translate loosely as sort, segregate, shine, standardize, and self-discipline.

fig. 35

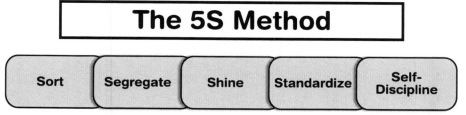

The 5S Method

| Sort | Segregate | Shine | Standardize | Self-Discipline |

Sort

The *sort* portion of the 5S method can be quickly summarized by the phrase "everything has a place." Sorting is a practical extension of the Lean focus on waste reduction. When a workstation or an employee's work area is "sorted," everything is in its place. Unnecessary items, or items that are not needed at hand, are stored properly. If disposal is required, then these items are disposed of properly.

These simple concepts can expand to encompass a diverse range of circumstances, objects, and materials. A sorted workplace is one that defies the accumulation of unwanted or waste materials. This means that there are fewer obstacles to productive flow—a workstation that is free of debris is an efficient workstation— and that waste material is removed from the production stream. This macro-scale concept trickles down to the very micro scale of employee workstations and even areas where employees may store personal effects, such as lockers and break areas.

Proper and thorough sorting does come with an administrative cost, however: it is necessary to constantly evaluate which items and materials are in fact necessary and which should be stored or disposed of. These evaluation activities are often carried out by a dedicated supervisor or frontline level leader and can take time away from other value-added activities. Additionally, if items are deemed "unnecessary" but are not waste or are not in need of disposal, then they must be stored correctly. This consumes space, time for transport, and time for the coordination of storage.

Storage areas should be red-tagged as necessary to prevent the accidental reintroduction of unnecessary materials and items back into the production stream, or to reinforce the fact that they are only needed in some circumstances.

The rationale for these costs and additional work, of course, is that overall productivity is increased and workflow is undisturbed through obstacle-free production. Sorting strives to reduce waste events across the board but focuses on reducing unevenness in workflow.

Segregate

The *segregate* aspect of the 5S method is the next logical step after sorting. While sorting identifies which items are necessary, segregation is the practice of organizing those items in such a way that they will produce the most efficient benefit. Segregation activities mean arranging tools so that the highest-use tools are closest at hand. It means ensuring that the people who have a constant or consistent need for tools and materials can easily locate and access those tools or materials, and that all of their work can be done in the most efficient manner possible.

Just like every other aspect of Lean, segregation is not a one-time activity. Segregation activities should regularly be subjected to PDCA-style review, and those employees responsible for segregation activities should be empowered to make changes as the need arises.

Sorting and segregation are interrelated processes, as are segregation and the next "S," shine. In one interpretation of the 5S method, segregation and shine are combined into a single activity, effectively producing an alternative 4S method. This is reflective of the kaizen approach that makes up the backbone of Lean methodology: always be improving, always be learning, and always be flexible.

If, in implementation, it makes more sense to aggregate 5S methodologies into single, hybrid activities, then that is what should be done. Stretching an organization to fit the Lean model is a backward approach and a losing proposition. Instead, Lean—and the 5S method—should be stretched and tweaked to fit the organization and its production activities, culture, and specific production processes.

Shine

Shine embodies the concept that cleanliness is next to godliness (so to speak). It is sometimes referred to as "sweep" or "scrub." Not only do employees who work in a clean and well-maintained workplace have more respect for their employer and their responsibilities, but there are a number of practical benefits of a continuous commitment to cleanliness.

Regular cleaning of workstations and equipment means that there are no barriers to efficient production and labor. Just as the 5S practice of sorting eliminates unnecessary objects and materials to ensure an even workflow, a clean and orderly workstation is always ready and easy to navigate. Regular cleaning is a preventative measure as well; it reduces the effects of wear and tear on equipment and can prolong the life of critical production components.

A clean work environment is also the foundation of a safe work environment. From the very rudimentary practices of cleaning spills and clearing debris that can cause slips, trips, and falls to the more advanced activities that ensure that safety equipment can work without impediment, cleanliness is a vital component of safety.

Cleaning activities can serve another purpose: cleaning as inspection. Thorough cleaning already takes a deep dive into equipment and workstations—why retrace your steps a second time for a follow-up inspection? Scheduling cleaning routines to coincide with maintenance inspections saves time and effort. Cleaning routines can also be employed to maintain and monitor other 5S method activities such as sorting and segregation.

The effectiveness of a rigorous shine program is often evaluated using the following phrase: "Anyone not familiar with the environment should be able to detect problems within 5 seconds from within 50 feet."

Standardize

Standardization is a common theme within the Lean framework. Standards provide benchmarks by which performance can be measured, and if performance can be measured, areas of opportunity for improvement can be identified (and improvement must be continuous). The standardize portion of 5S serves to ensure that all other 5S activities are targeted, productive, and goal-oriented.

Just as all the tools and equipment on the production line and at employee workstations must be in their places, so too must the 5S activities be organized and monitored. Standardization codifies best practices and maintains the organization's intent and standards in all aspects of deployment.

Self-Discipline

Self-Discipline, also known as "sustain", ties all of the other 5S activities together in a manner that is characteristic of the Lean framework. The definition, and therefore translation, of shitsuke, the fifth "S" in Japanese, is nuanced and complex. As a result, sustaining and self-discipline are both only parts of the concept behind the word.

Shitsuke can be defined in two ways. The first is more akin to discipline in the forceful sense of the word—it takes force to align all of the 5S methods into place. In this sense, the barriers of change are understood and described. Once these changes are in place, the second and more prevalent meaning of shitsuke becomes relevant. This is the process of self-discipline that is more in line with the English definition: the structured and conscious effort to maintain standards and practices. To do what is necessary "without being told."

The aim of this text is far from an exploration of Japanese language and culture, but the above example is instructive to students of the Lean philosophy in the idea that Lean is far more than simply a rulebook for productive and efficient manufacturing. Examples like the one above underscore the fact that Lean is a complete overhaul of an organization's culture and perspective, and it should be viewed as such.

A commitment to the letter of Lean while failing to commit to the spirit will only produce half-measures of success.

The Path to Implementation

The organization-wide implementation of Lean is not an undertaking to be considered lightly. While the tremendous gains that can be had through the adoption of Lean are enough to entice the management of any manufacturing concern, the process requires total organizational commitment, and in many cases a completely new way of thinking, a revised mindset, and a radically distinct corporate culture.

It is no surprise, then, that the checklist for Lean manufacturing implementation is a lengthy one. What follows is a broad strokes guide to the key components of an organizational shift to the Lean manufacturing framework. Keep in mind that, as with all dramatic change, benefits are not realized overnight. The kaizen method of improvement subscribes to the notion that the most impactful changes are executed in an incremental fashion with innovation in mind. Once the foundation is established, constant and vigilant incremental improvement and waste reduction measures achieve Toyota Production System levels of Lean achievement.

The Lean Manufacturing Implementation Road Map

1. **Key People** : Form a team to lead the charge. There should be a mix of Lean manufacturing specialists and those with general business experience. If no specialists exist within the organization, there is an entire industry of Lean consultants waiting to fill this role.

2. **Open Channel of Communication** : Establish an open channel of communication for everyone involved. This level of visibility is essential to successful implementation efforts and coordination of the "leap to Lean." Visibility within the initiative and transparency from outside the implementation team will help build trust throughout the ranks.

3. **Foundational Training** : This is the first round of immersion in the Lean philosophy. Focus first on the structure that makes up the Lean framework: the culture of kaizen; the elimination of muda, mura, and muri; the principles of PDCA; flexibility; etc. While more thorough training will be necessary for key players, every employee at all levels of the organization should be familiar with the foundational concepts of the Lean framework. The innovative properties of kaizen can only truly be implemented if staff from all levels understand their role within the contribution process.

4. **Facility Analysis** : Analyze existing facilities and layouts with a focus on the principles of Lean. Identify the difference between the production line's present state and a Lean-optimized state. This is an important step, as it informs future decisions.

5. **5S** : Begin application of the 5S methodology. The 5S method is a pillar of the workplace, and its deployment will build the habits, mindset, and best practices that are expanded upon for smooth Lean operations. This basic level of workplace organization helps lay the groundwork for future training and Lean best practices.

6. **Value Stream Mapping** : Map the current system as it is and determine points of waste throughout the system. Using value stream mapping tools, construct a comprehensive data picture of current operations so that goals for innovation may be set. Classify this waste with the D.O.W.N.T.I.M.E. eight sources of waste. Once identified and classified, future corrective action may be applied.

7. **Process Mapping** : While all processes may already be mapped, revisit the maps and remap processes with an eye for waste elimination. Extensive process mapping builds a benchmark against which all future innovation is measured.

8. **Takt Time Calculation** : Now that the processes are mapped and the value stream is mapped, some changes may already be underway. Calculate a takt time for each product. As operations improve, this time will shrink and produce consistent results, but as with process mapping, takt time—and its subsequent change—is a valuable benchmark metric.

9. **Determine Equipment Effectiveness** : Assess existing equipment with a structured and investigative approach. Undertake line balancing activities to work toward more even production.

10. **SMED** : Based on data gathered so far and on insights from the last step, apply Single Minute Exchange of Die practices to bring down the cost and duration of changeovers.

11. **Kanban** : Develop and introduce a kanban system into the production process. Analyze the continuous flow—replenishment of materials at the pace of production—and coordinate scheduling with a heijunka box.

12. **TQM** : Analyze production to ensure that quality control measures are in place and are effective. Implement poka-yoke measures to error-proof the production line.

13. **Cellular Flow** : Through informed innovation, move toward a cellular facility layout and uniform flow, shedding waste and inefficiency with each iteration of kaizen and innovation.

14. **Standardize** : Develop standardized operations to leverage the economies of repetition, and to simplify training and maximize efficiency and productivity. Standardization codifies gains and ensures that operations run smoothly.

15. **Continuous Improvement** : By this point it should be obvious that the path to Lean implementation is not a onetime activity. Kaizen, and the drive and need for innovation within a dynamic and fluid marketplace, should spur constant improvement and encourage organizations to welcome change.

fig. 36

The Lean Manufacturing Implementation Roadmap

1. Form a team to spearhead the initiative.

2. Establish clear channels of communication.

3. Execute foundational training to prime staff for more advanced concepts.

4. Analyze facilities with a focus on the current state versus an ideal Lean state.

5. Initiate 5S practices to organize the workplace in preparation for Lean production methods.

6. Perform value stream mapping with an eye for waste.

7. Perform detailed process mapping to establish a benchmark.

8. Calculate takt times for the elements of the product mix.

9. Evaluate equipment effectiveness and begin line balancing.

10. Begin SMED measures to increase production line flexibility.

11. Employ a kanban system coordinated by a heijunka box.

12. Focus on TQM practices to ensure quality control measures are in place.

13. Move facility layout to conform to efficient cellular flow.

14. Standardize practices to leverage economies of repetition and to sustain efficiency gains.

15. Embrace the kaizen culture in all forms to incrementally innovate while creating and maintaining competitive edge.

Implementation Concerns

The Lean business model is gaining popularity as an effective production tool, but it is not without downsides in implementation. As more companies begin implementation, some issues have arisen.

A frequent criticism is that planners implementing Lean focus on the tools and qualitative methods as opposed to the culture. The Lean business model is the "total package" in implementation, and while the tools and methods can be effectively used piecemeal, the true value of Lean exists in the kaizen culture that tirelessly strives for improvement. This scenario is often accompanied by implementation that has been attempted by firm management not entirely familiar with the top-to-bottom process.

Another issue that has become apparent is the decision by management to use a solution that they have determined without uncovering the true problem and without input from members of the production staff. This seems to be an "old habits die hard" scenario. True visibility within an organization and commitment to the practice of kaizen would utilize the input of the frontline workforce and observe the process at the production level, not from the boardroom. These conditions result in sound decision-making on paper, but solutions can fail to improve the problem or have the intended reduction result.

Additionally, practitioners of Lean tend to use the model as a "one size fits all" waste reduction program. This is usually not the case as the specific implementation changes from application to application. While the culture of kaizen and the concepts of differentiating between value-added and non-value-added activities are powerful enough to span diverse industries, some firms simply find that not every tool is needed. Implementation of a hybrid program that takes all of the beneficial parts of Lean and pairs them to the specific needs of the organization is the most effective use of the Lean model as opposed to a headfirst "leap to Lean."

The most significant implementation concern is the disruption of business activities due to systemic change. When an organization undergoes such a massive overhaul of people, processes, and values, the old ways of doing business are significantly disrupted. This disruption is a positive thing; if shedding wasteful and shortsighted business practices produces a more competitive Lean machine, then the net gains are significant.

This forward-looking mindset does not change the fact that Lean implementation can be costly and long, and can be accompanied by a significant learning curve while staff members acclimate to the new way of doing things. In the short term, operations can suffer huge disruption while the process is being implemented, but the long-term gains are well worth the cost if management is willing to ride out the short-term costs.

To Recap

- The Lean method places a high importance on respect for people. This dovetails cleanly with the concept of kaizen and the idea that the spark for innovation can truly come from any level of the organization.

- The 5S method is a process that helps clarify and codify the Lean organizational aspects of a well-organized workplace. It puts employees in the right mindset to carry out Lean activities and provides a process-based foundation for future Lean activities.

- The path to Lean implementation is not an easy one; often Lean methodologies represent a significant departure from traditional business practices. Concerns and barriers to adoption arise in the form of misplaced expectations on the part of management, costs of disruption due to change, and the mismatching of Lean tools and Lean philosophy. The Lean framework is best deployed all together, because each of the tools and principles builds on the others.

Key Questions (Answers on pg. 137)

1. Although an organization-wide respect for people is a positive goal, it is not an asset of kaizen culture.

   a) true   b) false

2. The 5S method includes which of the following process activities?

   a) sample   b) substitute
   c) standardize   d) support production

3. The 5S method is a process-oriented method of workplace organization.

   a) true   b) false

4. When implementing Lean across an entire organization, management can expect to see immediate return on their investment.

   a) true   b) false

5. Which of the following is a concern when implementing Lean across an organization?

a) the cost of retraining staff

b) a disconnect between the Lean philosophy and its practical tools

c) the impact and cost that disruption due to change can bring

d) all of the above

conclusion

The marketplace is changing. What was once the Toyota Production System has evolved into competitive-edge-generating protocol. It is difficult to foresee what the next level of business evaluation and production strategy will look like, but it is safe to say that the Lean business model and business models like it have paved the way. The power of kaizen culture and constant waste reduction spans a multitude of industries and has made its way into personal lives as well. Whether service oriented, manufacturing focused, financially motivated or construction minded, kaizen empowers each level and every member of an organization to promote and introduce innovation into everyday operations and business practices.

A focus on communication, visibility, and broad view strategy is also a powerful asset to any organization's corporate culture, both within and outside of the manufacturing sector. These tools help streamline "business as usual" operations and encourage examination of the enterprise's market position relative to competitors. This, coupled with a vigilant examination of processes for innovation and change, provides organizations with a "change is good" mindset. In a business environment where it is increasingly true that the only constant is change, an innovation- and change-focused enterprise will not only survive, but thrive.

In many ways the globe is shrinking; competition is becoming fiercer, new markets are more accessible, and new customers are presenting opportunities to be won or lost every day. Considering the nature of the modern business market, it is the opinion of this author that the concepts Lean uses to empower businesses are the foundation for effective, efficient, and harmonious commerce for the entire world and will be for years to come.

appendix
Value Stream Mapping Sample

Value stream mapping was touched on starting on page 55. The process can become quite complex and is very time-consuming. It is important to remember that effective value stream mapping requires a high degree of coordination between different workforce elements and a thorough understanding of and practical competence in the Lean methodology.

Value stream mapping is not for novice Lean enterprises. A well-developed level of trust between and among supervisors, operators, and upper management is necessary for effective and impactful value stream mapping. It is also important to keep in mind that value stream mapping—in the instances of both strategic and tactical use—may prompt decision makers to make a number of changes to processes, labor classifications, and existing layouts.

So why use a value stream map at all?

Value stream maps are first and foremost visibility and efficiency analysis tools. Areas of waste and inefficiency cannot be addressed if they are not made visible, and an effective value stream map does just that; it reveals challenges and barriers within a process or family of processes. In this capacity, a value stream map is a diagnostic tool that forms the basis of an improvement plan for a process.

Like a blueprint, decision makers can refer back to a value stream map as a sort of common language or starting point to inform their improvement endeavors. In this way, the VSM tool serves to increase the visibility and communication between different workforce elements as well; with a unified and common point of reference, collaboration is a smoother process.

Value stream maps are effective at the organizational and departmental levels for the aforementioned reasons; this macro-level visual representation also contains a snapshot of relevant metrics and a bird's-eye view of the process as a whole from start to finish. On a more micro scale they can also help individual operators, supervisors, and decision makers understand the relationships and flows of materials, labor, and information, and the work-in-progress that responds to customer demand.

When analyzing a process and identifying the goals of value stream mapping efforts, common process issues that require elimination or reduction include the following:

Excessive DOWNTIME waste such as waiting, motion, or inventory. This *muda* could be in the form of too many handoffs, unneeded approvals, or the wasteful duplication of work—all of which can be identified through the analysis of an effective value stream map. Dead zones in the process flow can also be identified. Dead zones are areas throughout the process where work gets held up or lost, or where overall process flow is disrupted. In total, any lost time, wasted effort, and other non-value-added activities become much more visible through the value stream mapping process.

VSMs are both strategic and tactical tools. When created to analyze and design an ideal "future state" of a process, the map itself is a strategic tool. Here decision makers and members of management can make a wish list of what they would like to see in the improved version of the process. Once the value stream map has been analyzed, the resulting implementation plans aiming to arrive at the ideal future state of the process are tactical tools. Based on interpretations of the data recorded in the VSM, these plans are often tailored in the micro scale.

Step 1 : Select a Product or Service Family

The product/service family grid can be a helpful tool here. The objective of step one is to set the ground rules for all of the mapping efforts to follow. In addition to selection of the product family—and therefore the processes that will be mapped—the scope of mapping efforts, roles and responsibilities of those involved, and which general goals should be achieved.

Examining the "future state" of a process also means defining its current state. These future state conceptions can be drawn upon to inform the scope and goal of value stream mapping efforts. In short, a business case must be made for value stream mapping efforts—it is, after all, an expensive and time-consuming process.

In addition to identifying the scope, process boundaries should be identified, as well as differences in value and waste between the current state and the ideal future state. This examination can be classified overall as a design phase, and design tools (such as DMADV) may be applicable for some teams.

When defining boundaries—both the boundaries of the entire process and those of its component steps—a logical starting point is to select points within the process where inputs (raw materials or the work-in-process from the prior workstation) cannot be returned to the previous step. Correctly and satisfactorily defining each step of the process will simplify matters down the road.

Step 2 : Start with the Process Flow

To map the process at its basis, the process flow is first recorded. Every effort should be made to ensure that the process is captured as true to life as possible. This often means doing things the old-fashioned way: with graph paper, a pencil, and a stopwatch.

A good rule of thumb when capturing process data for mapping is to never record information not personally seen. Look at average performance, and rule out clear exceptions that could skew overall interpretation of the process as a whole.

It is important to start with an accurate foundation for this stage and for the stages that follow. It is also important to use a key of standardized icons like the legend pictured below to make the final product truly part of the common language of value stream mapping. If a finished VSM was constructed using icons and flowchart symbols that only the mapping team understood, then each new person who had to interpret the map would need a lesson on which symbols represented what components of the mapped process. A good rule of thumb is to stick to the commonly accepted symbols—but always keep a key handy.

fig. 37

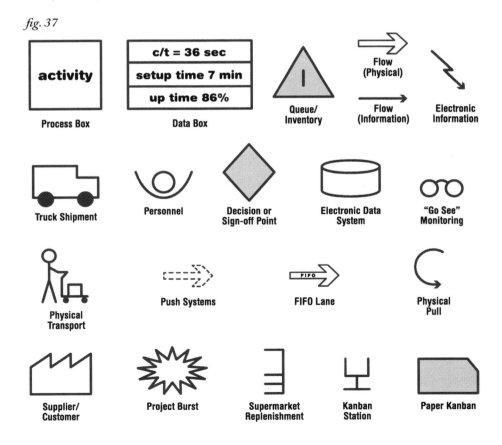

The process map is constructed in the same direction that demand travels through the value stream itself—starting with the customer and working "backward" toward suppliers. To verify that the process has been completely captured, a SIPOC diagram of the process is a useful checklist, both in the process mapping stage and throughout the remaining stages of the VSM construction. Essentially a blank flowchart for the process at hand, the process map stage is pictured below.

fig. 38

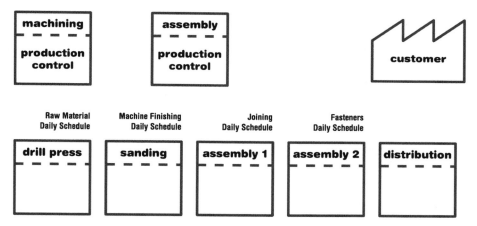

Step 3 : Add the Flow of Materials

The process flow acts as a foundation and basis for the finished value stream map. The material flow step and the following steps are constructed as overlays for the original process map. This fact serves to further underscore the necessity of producing a process map that is an accurate capture of the true-to-life process as it is actually carried out.

Here the flows of all materials are added to the process map. In the case of complex product families with divergent and convergent material flows, group the flows of similar materials together for the sake of simplicity, but don't lose detail in the process. If a material flow is divergent in the actual process, then on the value stream map it should also be represented as such.

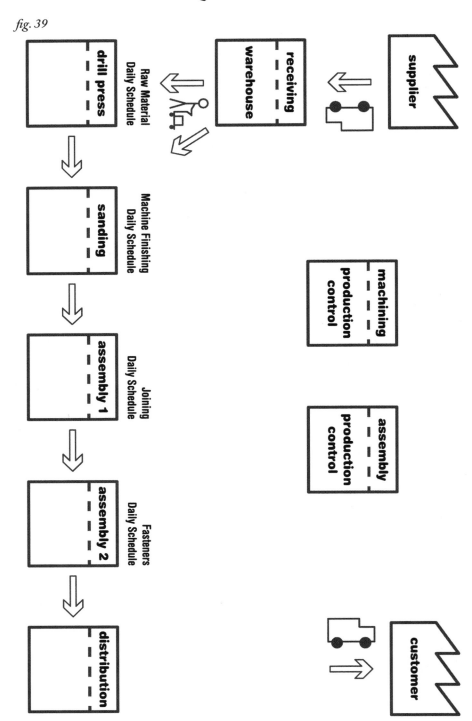

fig. 39

This mapping step also includes the activities that are associated with the flow of materials and interact with it directly; this could include sampling, testing, quality control points, and other analysis measures (see figure 39).

Step 4 : Add the Flow of Information Overlay

Added as another overlay, the visual representation of the flows of information across the value stream is the next component in the mapping process. All forms of communication and information flows are relevant to this mapping stage, but especially the methods by which different elements of the value stream communicate with one another, specifically how the whole process communicates with supplier(s) and customer(s).

Scheduling, scheduling methods, and the way in which they interact with the workstations and flows that they impact are also critical components of the information flow overlay. Despite the fact that the "flow of information" can sometimes be an abstract concept, it can still be mapped, visualized, and analyzed. Activities that meet those three criteria are also visible, and true to Lean, Lean Six Sigma, and the practice of value stream mapping visibility leads to action (see figure 40).

Step 5 : Add Relevant Process Data

Process data is critical to understanding the actual characteristics of flow through the process. The data collected in this stage will inform the next one, so just as with each one of the preceding stages, accuracy and a true-to-life capture of data is of paramount importance.

The specific process data that is relevant to the goals of value stream mapping can vary slightly with decision maker preference, the nature of the process—for example temperature may be a relevant metric for some processes and irrelevant for others—and the complexity of operations.

fig. 40

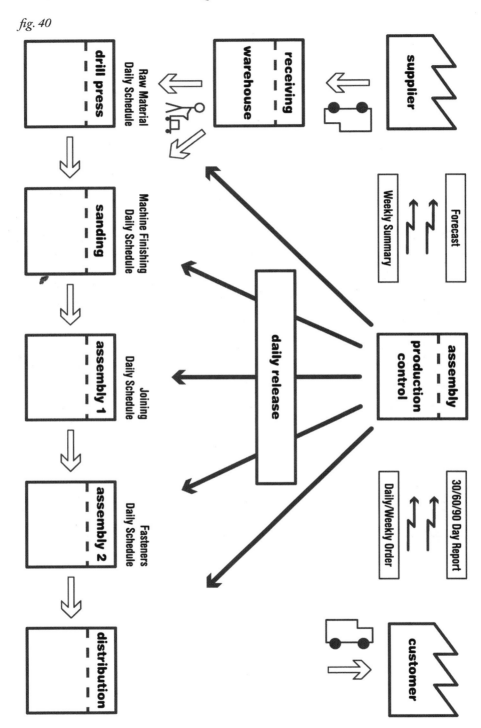

A good rule of thumb is to collect data regarding the following process aspects:

- Trigger (what initiates the step as defined by its boundaries)
- Setup time
- Processing time per unit
- Takt time (this is a measurement of customer demand)
- Scrap rate (the measure of defect rate or defective production)
- Number of people
- Downtime (expressed as a percentage)
- Work-in-progress both down and upstream
- Cost of links (examples include links to the supplier, the warehouse, to IT, et cetera)
- Batch size

Step 6 : Add Process & Lead Time

Lead time has such an outsized impact on business decisions and operations that its importance cannot be overstated. Lead time impacts delivery time, which impacts the creation of value for the customer (late delivery is not valuable) and customer satisfaction. Lead time is a massive factor in scheduling, and controlling lead time is the core of Just-in-Time production and inventory methods.

The most widely accepted convention for recording process and lead time is with the sawtooth timeline (figure 41). Here, production lead time is shown on the "peaks" of the timeline, and the processing time per unit is recorded in the "valleys" of the line. There is, however, no universally accepted standard to this component of a value stream map, and therefore some organizations and decision makers have developed their own methods.

Due to some confusion over the sawtooth-style timelines, some organizations simply use a straight line with lead time listed on the top of the line and process time listed below (with the two values vertically

fig. 41

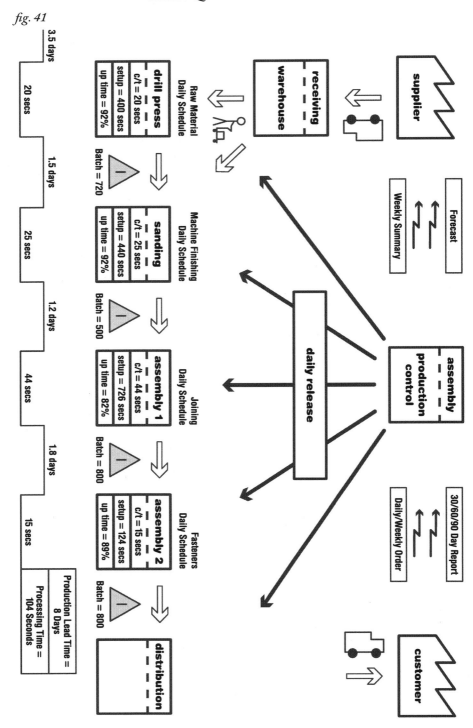

aligned). This prevents potential instances of team members accidentally transposing the two values. Other decision makers have chosen to simply focus on different measures altogether, such as production lead time and VAT (value-added time).

Step 7 : Verify the Map with Non-Familiar Staff

The last step of the value stream mapping process is the independent verification stage. It's a mandatory "extra set of eyes," especially eyes that are not familiar with the process. Here it is absolutely critical that universal value stream mapping symbols have been used, because the test of an effective value stream map is that uninitiated staff can read and correctly draw the appropriate insights from the completed map.

Suppliers and customers should also be consulted, if possible, to ensure that the VSM is as accurate and true to life as possible. If errors are detected in this stage, the problem must be resolved before tactical improvement plans are formulated that rely on the data included in the finished value stream map.

glossary

5M-
the 5 M's of manufacturing. The 5 M's represent the primary categories of causal effects that should be considered when brainstorming potential causes for inclusion in a fishbone diagram. The 5 M's are as follows: machine, method, material, manpower, and measurement.

5S Method-
a process-oriented program of workplace organization. The 5S method standardizes best practices for the efficient execution of day-to-day activities. The 5 S's are as follows: sort, segregate, shine, standardize, and self-discipline.

5W1H-
a structured investigative method used to determine the root cause of an issue. The process uses a successive series of "why" questions to bring hidden causal effects to the surface.

A3 Problem Solving Method-
a practical application of the PDCA process improvement and problem solving method. Using a single piece of ISO A3-sized paper (11"x17"), the focus of problems is narrowed, and a structured investigative approach can be applied.

Buffer Inventory-
see Safety Stock.

Bullwhip Effect-
the concept that miscommunication amplifies disruption and variation throughout the supply chain and throughout an organization. When one department gets a garbled message, they are likely to distort it to the next department and so on until it reaches the final recipient, where the message is completely distorted.

Cellular Facility Layout-
a facility layout that aims for maximum flexibility and efficiency by combining aspects of the product-oriented facility layout and the process-oriented facility layout. Clusters of workstations are organized into "product families" and then designed to fit the process layout.

Core Competency-
a set of business operations at which a particular organization excels. A core competency is the foundational component of competitive edge.

D.O.W.N.T.I.M.E.-
an acronym used to help remember the eight sources of physical waste (muda): defective production, overprocessing, waiting, non-used employee talent, inventory, motion, and excessive production.

Decision Point Analysis-
a tool primarily used by organizations utilizing a "T" configuration production scheme. This mapping tool identifies the point at which pull demand (actual customer demand) gives way to demand that has been forecasted (artificial demand).

Outsource Decision Matrix-
a tool used to identify processes, activities, and tasks that are candidates for outsourcing through the comparison of criticality and impact.

Demand Amplification Mapping-
also known as Forrester Effect Mapping, demand amplification mapping is a visual tool used to identify the distortion that occurs between different supply chain entities within the value stream.

Economies of Repetition-
the concept that the repetition of specific activities and processes increases efficiency over time.

Economies of Scale-
the microeconomic concept that as the size and output of a manufacturing operation increases, costs can be spread out over more units, thereby reducing the cost to produce each unit. Economies of scale is a large cost reduction driver of push production and large batch manufacturing.

E-Kanban-
the electronic integration of a kanban system into an organization's ERP (enterprise resource planning) software. E-kanban systems generally cost more to implement, but have unprecedented levels of visibility and do not suffer from the disruptions of lost, illegible, or damaged kanban cards.

External Setup Operations-
line changeover setup operations that can be performed while the production machine is still running. This is much more desirable than changeovers that require machine shutdown (internal setup operations) because the production line can continue to move while adjustments are taking place.

Fixed Position Facility Layout-
a facility layout method best employed when the product in question is so large or heavy that workstations move around the product rather than the product moving around the workstation.

Forrester Effect Mapping-
see Demand Amplification Mapping.

Heijunka Box-
a visual scheduling tool that uses a grid-like construction to organize various kanban control cards by their various stages within the production process. An essential tool to promote even production flow, heijunka boxes are a critical scheduling component of kanban implementation.

Internal Setup Operations-
line changeover operations that require that the production machine be shut down, thus causing stoppage on the production line. The Single Minute Exchange of Die method seeks to reduce this disruption by converting internal setup operations into external ones.

Inventory-
the total on-hand store of goods, materials, and supplies. For production operations, production inventory is broken into three stages: raw materials, work in progress, and finished goods.

Ishikawa Diagrams-
cause-and-effect diagrams that are used to investigate and determine the root causes of a specific effect impacting a process at hand. Also known as fishbone diagrams.

IVAT Analysis-
see Production Variety Funnel.

Just-in-Time-
a method of cost reduction through the elimination of carrying inventory. Just-in-Time protocols ensure that only the amount of materials needed for production are transported, and that they arrive exactly when needed. On the finished goods side of production, JIT methods produce small batches that are a close match for customer demand, and are scheduled and produced in such a way that the manufacturer never has to carry inventory.

Kaizen-
the implementation of a culture of constant improvement, and a central theme of the Lean philosophy and business model. Kaizen is built on the premise that continual, incremental change causes the least amount of disruption, and that change can build upon other, previous changes to create innovation and competitive edge. Kaizen values the input of employees at all levels of the organization, recognizing that the spark of innovation can come from anywhere.

Kanban-
a flow-oriented method of material and goods coordination and replenishment. Based on the shelf-stocking methods of supermarkets, kanban operations simultaneously move products through the value stream while replenishing the materials that were consumed through production.

Lag Measures-
metrics and insights that can be gathered after the fact. Lag measures represent the feedback portion of a closed-loop system.

Lean Six Sigma-
a hybrid business management system that includes components from both Lean Manufacturing and Six Sigma Quality. Lean Six Sigma offers a total package of production optimization, quality control, waste reduction, and competitive edge.

Machine (5M)-
a causal category for the construction of fishbone diagrams. The machine category encompasses any equipment related to the process at hand. This includes computer systems and production tools primarily, but also extends to all tools that may be a part of the production process.

Manpower (5M)-
a causal category for the construction of fishbone diagrams. The manpower category encompasses any people who might have a causal impact on the process at hand.

Material (5M)-
a causal category for the construction of fishbone diagrams. The material category encompasses any and all materials that are involved in the production cycle and that may have a causal impact on the process at hand.

Measurement (5M)-
a causal category for the construction of fishbone diagrams. The measurement category encompasses any and all measurements and data collection that may occur in regard to the process at hand. This includes the accuracy of observations, thoroughness of investigations, and the calibration of data-gathering equipment.

Method (5M)-
a causal category for the construction of fishbone diagrams. The method category encompasses the total sum of protocols, process design, and methodology employed for the execution of the process at hand.

Muda-
one of the three overall sources of waste, muda represents physical waste events. All physical waste events can be traced back to the D.O.W.N.T.I.M.E. eight sources of waste.

Mura-
one of the three overall sources of waste, mura represents waste in the form of unevenness of production, or unequal production loading.

Muri-
one of the three overall sources of waste, muri represents waste in the form of overburden or a failure to understand production capacity.

Net Available Time to Work-
a component of takt time calculation. The total amount of time that is available for production activities, less breaks and other nonproduction time set aside for business activities.

Non-Value-Added-
activities that do not produce value that can be passed along to the customer. Non-value-added events are considered waste, and the Lean philosophy relentlessly works to not only differentiate value-added from non-value-added activities, but to reduce the impact that non-value-added activities (waste events) have on business processes.

Outsourcing-
the process of assigning business activities to a third party vendor or business with the intent of leveraging the economies of core competency or cost reduction.

PDCA-
a problem-solving and process-improvement process that focuses on creating actionable feedback. Plan, Do, Check, Adjust (or Act), also known as the Deming Cycle, has a wide variety of applications not only across the Lean business model but across a variety of industries.

Physical Structure Mapping-
an overview of an entire supply chain that is generated based on its physical structure. The physical structure map can be constructed either by visualizing cost centers or through volume-based mapping.

Poka-Yoke-
intentional constraints that are introduced into operations to reduce defective production due to human error. These "foolproofing" measures turn normal operations activities into processes, improving teachability and leveraging the economies of repetition.

Process Activity Mapping-
a narrower look at the components of a value stream. This tool dissects and maps individual processes as opposed to the entire value stream.

Process Facility Layout-
a facility layout that favors products with low volumes and high levels of differentiation. Under this facility layout protocol, workstations and resources are grouped based on the various paths that produce the product variants.

Product Facility Layout-
a facility layout that is ideal for mass production—high volumes of products with little or no differentiation. This facility layout is most closely associated with traditional manufacturing, the push production system, and the economies of scale.

Production Leveling-
the process of reducing the creation of waste events due to unevenness of production flow. Production leveling can be performed on the production side of the equation as well as the demand side to introduce evenness into production.

Production Variety Funnel-
also known as an IVAT analysis, the production variety funnel analysis identifies which set of manufacturing models the production of a particular product conforms to. Once the mode of production has been identified, specific and known traits and protocols can be applied to the production of goods.

Pull Production System-
the opposite of the push production system, the pull production system focuses on customer demand. As demand is generated, materials and goods are "pulled" into the production cycle, and in this way production matches demand as demand changes. The pull production system, when working in tandem with many of Lean's flexible manufacturing methods, creates a responsive production process that matches demand and does not carry excess inventory or generate waste through the production of large batches.

Push Production System-
the traditional approach to manufacturing whereby artificial demand is "pushed" through the production cycle. Large batches of goods are stored in anticipation of forecasted sales. Leveraging the economies of scale, costs are spread out over a high number of units, bringing the unit cost down and picking up the slack of this high-waste system.

Quality Filter Mapping-
a visual tool that identifies areas where quality issues exist within a value stream. With the deployment of this method, three sources of insufficient quality can be identified: product defects, service defects, and internal scrap.

Raw Materials-
the basic materials from which finished goods are made. This unfinished material is generally assumed to be homogeneous and comprises the raw materials portion of production inventory (raw materials, work in progress, finished goods).

Safety Stock-
a buffer to insulate inventory levels from fluctuations in demand. Safety stock is a characteristic of the push production system, where artificial demand is "pushed" through the production process. Conversely, the pull production system's flexibility and focus on actual demand eliminates the need for, and cost of carrying, safety stock.

Segregate (5S)-
a component of the 5S method, segregation is the next logical step after sorting. Once materials and tools have been examined and determined to be relevant to the process at hand, they are organized (or segregated) to ensure that they are available in an efficient manner.

Self-Discipline (5S)-
a component of the 5S method, self-discipline (also known as "sustain") is the structured and conscious effort to maintain the rigors of the 5S method and sustain the gains afforded by its implementation.

Shine (5S)-
a component of the 5S method, shine reflects all of the positive aspects of maintaining a clean and orderly workplace. From employee confidence and respect to reduced safety hazards, a clean workplace is an efficient one.

Single Minute Exchange of Die (SMED)-
a flexibility and cost-cutting program that strives to reduce the line changeover time to a single digit number of minutes. This radically increases the flexibility and responsiveness of production and reduces levels of waste. Mastering SMED within an organization is a critical component of a highly developed and flexible pull production system.

Six Sigma Quality-
a process-improvement and quality-focused business management method that uses statistical tools to improve productivity and quality throughout. Many of the tools available within the Six Sigma system can be used in tandem with the Lean philosophy and toolkit, producing the hybrid business improvement method Lean Six Sigma.

Small Lot Production-
a feature of the pull production system that focuses on waste reduction and flexibility through the production of batches that meet demand instead of large batches that are based on artificial demand and are "pushed" through production.

Sort (5S)-
a part of the 5S framework, the concept of a sorted workspace determines the most expedient and useful places for objects, tools, materials, and goods.

Spaghetti Plot-
a visual map of data that can be expressed as flows. Also known as workflow charts, spaghetti plots are used to track the movements of people and goods to determine more efficient layouts.

Standardization (5S)-
a part of the 5S framework, standardization seeks to transform activities into processes so that they can benefit from the economies of repetition.

Supply Chain Responsiveness Matrix-
a visual tool that analyzes an organization's lead time and inventory levels. The resulting graph highlights areas where slow-moving stock is concentrated.

Takt Time-
a measure of unit production time relevant to the rate of customer demand. While the product of a takt time is expressed as a certain number of parts per period, this is a measure of flow and may not reflect the actual duration of production for each unit.

Theory of Constraints (TOC)-
a systems improvement model that is built on the basic assumption that every system is subject to at least one constraint that creates a bottleneck. Once this constraint has been broken, the system will become more efficient, but is now subject to another, new limiting factor. This system is helpful for determining areas of inefficiency within operations, and assessing the best methods to effect change.

Total Quality Management (TQM)-
a unifying principle that underscores the interdependent relationship between the voice of the customer, the tools and processes used to manufacture goods, and the manner in which demand "pulls" goods through production.

Toyota Production System-
the set of principles, methods, and tools established by the Japanese vehicle manufacturer Toyota. The strides made by the Toyota company revolutionized and supercharged the Japanese economy, and the effective methods employed by Toyota have evolved into the versatile Lean Manufacturing system that we know today.

Tunnel Vision-
a singular focus on one goal at the expense of visibility of others or the whole picture.

Value Stream-
the total sum of effort, operations, processes, and production that contributes to the creation of value for a customer. Value stream doesn't begin and end with the manufacturing organization. It begins with the customer and works backward through the supply chain, all the way upstream to the point of origin.

Value Stream Mapping-
a Lean toolkit that is used to assess the current state of all activities and processes associated with production operations. The application of value stream mapping is designed to highlight areas where improvement is possible, and to differentiate value-added activities from waste, all while establishing a benchmark against which all improvement activities can be measured.

Value-Added-

activity that incurs costs that can be passed on to the customer (creates value). The Lean method's focus on the Voice of the Customer is a core driver of the need to differentiate value-added and non-value-added activities. Through various improvement methods, operations are trimmed of non-value-added activities (waste) and streamlined to only the necessary value-added processes.

Waste-

non-value-added activity. Waste incurs cost but does not produce value, so these costs cannot be passed on to the customer. Waste is represented within the Lean manufacturing system as falling under the categories of physical waste, unevenness of production, or overburden of production. In all aspects of Lean, the elimination of waste is a focal point of improvement activities.

answers

Chapter One
1d, 2b, 3b, 4b, 5a

Chapter Two
1c, 2b, 3b, 4a, 5d, 6b, 7b, 8c

Chapter Three
1d, 2d, 3b, 4a, 5c

Chapter Four
1b, 2c, 3a, 4b, 5d

references

Fantin, Ivan. 2014. *Applied Problem Solving. Method, Applications, Root Causes, Countermeasures, Poka-Yoke and A3*. Milan, Italy: Createspace.

George, Michael L., David Rowlands, Mark Price, and John Maxey. 2005. *The Lean Six Sigma Pocket Toolbook*. New York: McGraw-Hill.

Hirano, Hiroyuki. 1995. *5 Pillars of the Visual Workplace*. Cambridge: Productivity Press.

Ishikawa, Kaoru. 1976. *Guide to Quality Control*. Asian Productivity Organization.

Jacob, Dee, Suzan Bergland, and Jeff Cox. 2010. *Velocity*. New York: Free Press.

Laraia, Anthony C., Patricia E. Moody, and Robert W. Hall. 1999. *The Kaizen Blitz: Accelerating Breakthroughs in Productivity and Performance*. New York: John Wiley and Sons.

Lubben, R.T. 1988. *Just-in-Time Manufacturing: An Aggressive Manufacturing Strategy*. New York: McGraw-Hill.

Ohno, Taiichi. 1988. *Toyota Production System: Beyond Large-Scale Production*. Productivity Press.

Rother, Mike. 2009. *Toyota Kata: Managing People for Continuous Improvement and Superior Results.* New York: McGraw-Hill.

Rother, Mike, and John Shook. 2003. *Learning to See: Value-Stream Mapping to Create Value and Eliminate Muda.* Brookline: Lean Enterprise Institute.

Shingo, Shigeo. 1989. *A Study of the Toyota Production System.* Productivity Press.

about clydebank

We are a multimedia publishing company that provides reliable, high-quality, and easily accessible information to a global customer base. Developed out of the need for beginner-friendly content that can be accessed across multiple platforms, we deliver unbiased, up-to-date, information through our multiple product offerings.

Through our strategic partnerships with some of the world's largest retailers, we are able to simplify the learning process for customers around the world, providing our readers with an authoritative source of information for the subjects that matter to them. Our end-user focused philosophy puts the satisfaction of our customers at the forefront of our mission. We are committed to creating multimedia products that allow our customers to learn what they want, when they want, and how they want.

ClydeBank Finance is a division of the multimedia-publishing firm ClydeBank Media. ClydeBank Media's goal is to provide affordable, accessible information to a global market through different forms of media such as eBooks, paperback books and audio books. Company divisions are based on subject matter, each consisting of a dedicated team of researchers, writers, editors and designers.

For more information, please visit us at :
www.clydebankmedia.com
or contact *info@clydebankmedia.com*

Your world, simplified.

notes

Made in the USA
Middletown, DE
25 April 2019